MIDWEST SWEET BAKING HISTORY

MIDWEST SWEET BAKING HISTORY

Delectable Classics around Lake Michigan

Jenny Lewis

THE
History
PRESS

Published by The History Press

Charleston, SC 29403

www.historypress.net

Cover images: Images are from the author's private collection, with the exception of the

Washburn-Crosby Company advertisement from the late 1880s.

Cover design by Karleigh Hambrick.

First published 2011

ISBN 978-1-5402-3054-6

Library of Congress CIP data applied for.

Notice: The information in this book is true and complete to the best of our knowledge. It is offered without guarantee on the part of the author or The History Press. The author and The History Press disclaim all liability in connection with the use of this book.

CONTENTS

CONTENTS

FOREWORD

The American experience is laden with foods both surprising and clever, especially from strapped or mundane circumstances. Legends of gold miners sleeping on pillowed saddlebags, diligently cradling their sourdough starters beneath them for the next day's breakfast (Silver Dollar Pancakes), of a bread named for a woman who fed her husband nothing but molasses and cornmeal all day (Anadama/Anna Damn Her!) and of mock-custard pie so good that flies were attracted in droves (Shoo-Fly Pie) all conjure foods that seem to wink and smile at us—or at least promise a good story.

Immigrants and Americans have crisscrossed the United States so rapidly, with on-the-spot adaptations of old food traditions and clever ideas, many have been able to provide an income and future for their children in starting businesses from the ground up. The breathtaking speed with which we have filled our national table tells the tale of endless acres of farms speedily harvested. Our foodways have become "fast," so much so that it is a unique style of eating, our truly American heritage. Fast food in the United States carried the charm of a "fast" life. Our personal memories of fast food might be framed by a car window through which food arrived neatly wrapped before we sped away to newer and more novel experiences day after day. Every colorful meal implied a gift or an occasion, and we peered into the folds of paper expectantly. But one of the biggest accomplishments of the great industrial food system was that there was no "surprise." The food looked identical each and every time.

One can drive past "ghost" foodways left behind by the prominence of the fast-food industry in the middle states, such as the railroad lines crowding toward the historic Chicago Union Stockyards, now dusty and bare, the crowds of animals in

2,300 pens nearly forgotten. Nine million animals were butchered on the site yearly, which satisfied 80 percent of America's overall meat consumption. Today, the only remnant of the stockyards is a huge gate crowned with the head of "Sherman," a prize-winning bull that once overlooked the animals teeming below. The surrounding neighborhood seems incongruous, unsure—there may be ghosts of cattle running the streets at night. But the allure lives on; the name is a Chicago original, and many young artists are renovating factories in the district. Their start-up businesses proudly state a location in Chicago's "Back of the Yards" neighborhood, as if to resurrect it. And today, just down Halsted Street, chefs are shaping a smaller, less industrial foodway— their "local" restaurants have begun growing their own produce on rooftops and making their own cheese.

Today, we seek chefs who promise us foods that heal the land. Some cooks and chefs have the insights of social anthropologists, excavating and rediscovering the sanctity and meaning of food. In this style, Jenny Lewis's book traces authentic American middle state sweet baking, built out of ingredients and techniques from immigrants and entrepreneurs at their stoves.

Her book travels a luscious landscape; a vast array of indigenous ingredients is brought into the menu, from pecans to maple sugar and cranberries. Farmers, home bakers, ingredient companies and industrial bakeries are interwoven in relationships that speed up and bring forth exciting and creative recipes and inventions. Innovations such as baking powder, beet sugar and evaporated milk are explained in the environment of history, with its wars, social shifts and politics.

This is a wonderful trail, and Jenny is a most generous, insightful host for the story of *Midwest Sweet Baking History: Delectable Classics Around Lake Michigan.*

Heidi Hedeker
MA/MSW
Pastry Chef Instructor
Kendall College, Chicago, Illinois

PREFACE

It is not so strange that I, someone with immigrant roots springing from the Irish famine of the 1840s, should have chosen a profession in food, nor that I would want to record the immigrant obsession with food and the future of America, satisfying a need in the history of food. Simultaneously, though, it is about satisfying our immigrant heart as the storyteller relates the energy, industry and imagination of Americans.

I am a fifth-generation Chicagoan, and yet I have only one "remembered" recipe from my Irish American family: Christmas Whiskey Cake. My Irish ancestors did not come here with a trunk full of recipes or a tin full of seeds for planting. Rather, they brought with them memories of hunger and dreams of fantasy cakes and sugarplums. Most especially, they carried with them hope in an emerging nation that would embrace many food traditions, religions and nationalities to become America, their sweet home.

My goal is to follow the path of the sweet-toothed Americans in the middle states by means of history, recipes and true stories. The history of sweet baking in America is a big story. I hope to take a small slice of that bigger story here in the middle states. I have specifically taken Lake Michigan as my centering point, collecting stories from the states that border it: Wisconsin, Illinois, Indiana and Michigan.

This specific landscape surrounding Lake Michigan in pioneer times was the land of prairie, forests and Native Americans. To the eye of the immigrant, its tangled vastness and possibilities were limitless. One could say that landscape dominates desire. But in this case, the wild landscape unleashed the energy and the will of the immigrants to convert wilderness to homestead.

Collecting the oral history of contemporary bakers, as well as people working with ingredients for sweet bakers, has been an honor. In reflecting on their own work, many of them fell into line with those early immigrants who had a story to tell, and they often told it through their work and their love of food, as well as recipes and ingredients.

Acknowledgements

My first thanks are to my family, for after all, they are my immigrant foodways. Afternoon tea with scones and shortbreads gave my palate a move in the direction for baking. Growing up in the states surrounding Lake Michigan, I never questioned the bountiful harvests—fruits, corn, berries and wheat. Vacations on back roads yielded roadside foods for sale—maple syrup, pies, pasties, jams, jellies, doughnuts and more! Somehow food has always been in my life and on my mind, from grinding wheat for bread as a child to piping the cannoli at my first bakery job. Food symbolized happiness, sharing and the delight of meeting many new people.

I am honored to have had this opportunity to have met such wonderful people in these middle states. The stories collected in this text represent just a few of the amazing people living and contributing to our sweet baking foodways. I have always been of the mindset to disprove the meat-and-potato theory that claims that the people in the middle of America are plain folk. I hope that this material will disprove that; after all, look what has originated and derived from this landscape.

A special thank-you to Lexington College and its continued support through this project, especially our librarian, Mrs. Josephine Kujawa. Her weekly research updates kept the project on task. Chef Heidi Hedeker's baking affiliations and creations still continue to amaze me. As I finish this project, I am still thinking of my next sweet taste!

Sweet Baking Observed

The history of sweet baking is immense, but some points are necessary to recognize. The origins of sweet baking date back thousands of years. One would have to say that the "sweet" part was natural honey and fruit or fruit mashed into a paste and that the "baking" part might have been some type of bread. This type of combination was true in many parts of the world.

By the 1400s, in western Europe, the French pastry chefs were uniquely forming guild-unions that gave new meaning to the term "sweet baking." They took pastry making away from the baker's guild. Sweet baking then became a formal industry.

A key turning point in sweet history was when Christopher Columbus brought sugar cane with him to the Americas. Outlying islands proved to be a most perfect climate for production, but it was slow to grow on the mainland. By the seventeenth and eighteenth centuries, sugar refineries took the sugar cane and beet to a new level of availability.

The American Midwest sweet baking story I am telling deals with immigrants and sweet baking traditions—their encounters with new peoples, new ingredients and new inventions. It prods the history of the nation as well. Over time, the sweet flavors of the middle states found favor at home as the Lake Michigan states formed their own foodways.

INTRODUCTION

The four states surrounding Lake Michigan—Michigan, Indiana, Illinois and Wisconsin—carry the history of many immigrant groups. Each ethnic wave of settlers brought its own traditions and customs. Food was among the top priorities of daily life. How would they survive in this new land? The terrain was vast, it looked remarkably fertile and it was often inexpensive or even free for some homesteaders.

But the immigrants encountered natives already living in the forests and on the prairies who had established routines of life: hunting, gathering and agriculture. Some of the plants were also strange, like corn and cranberries, and some foods that the immigrants expected, like wheat, were not there and did not grow well when first planted.

In survival mode, the French, Scotch-Irish, Swedes, Germans, Bohemians and more held on to their own particular customs, gathering in ethnic enclaves or farming communities. But from the natives they learned new ways to hunt, gather and farm.

Ethnic foods and traditions had traveled with the immigrants to their new homes. But the plants and seeds brought from the homeland did not always yield the same results in the New World. New recipes developed. This need for adaption was somewhat of an obstacle to satisfying the sweet-toothed Europeans.

This short history describes the immigrants' learning curve. They mixed and matched recipes and ingredients. They tried new tastes, and they brought new tastes to the Native Americans. From johnny cakes to bannock and Twinkies, I will trace sweet baking developments in this territory. Beginning in the 1600s up to the present, you will see how this Lake Michigan–centered region contributed to Midwest sweet baking history.

PART I
LAKE MICHIGAN STATES SWEET BAKING

Chapter 1

Ꞑavigating the Early ꞩears

First Encounters

In the 1600s, the Lake Michigan region was populated by various Native American "woodland" tribes, most of whom were from Algonquin stock. They were hunter-gatherers but also farmers. Corn, beans and squash were the main crops, though other vegetables were also available, along with nuts, fruits and maple syrup. Their tribal boundaries were semipermanent. This area around Lake Michigan had a denser population than other regions of North America, and as tribes grew and shrank, moved forward or retreated, the boundaries shifted. The Native Americans lived life specific to the yield of nature's food.

Not every tribe was identical in its existence. The majority of this territory was covered with dense forest, and the natives survived by hunting, but not all Indians necessarily planted crops. Agricultural crops depended on how far north they lived, as well as the number of days of sun. Summer homes were built and crops tended.

The Wisconsin tribes—Chippewa, Dakota, Fox, Iowa, Kickapoo, Mohican, Miami, Munsee, Iroquois, Oto, Ottawa, Potawatomi, Tionontati, Winnebago and Wyandot—lived life seasonally. Nature's rhythm yielded an abundance of food: wild game, fish, corn, wild rice, squash, nuts and berries. Syrup and sugar from the maple trees were essential and labor-intensive.

Illinois territory was a prairie state except to the south, where the Mississippi and Ohio Rivers joined. The Illinois tribes—Illini, Kickapoo, Sauk, Fox, Iroquois, Chippewa, Ottawa, Potawatomi, Kaskasika, Miami and Shawnee—also lived according to a yearly cycle. Crops of corn, beans and squash are examples of plantings. Groups also gathered hickory nuts, black walnuts and pecans, as well as pawpaw fruit, grapes, plums and wild strawberries. Buffalo and wild game were hunted. Here, too, maples were also used for syrup and sugar. Even roots and herbs were part of their foodways, with wintergreen and sassafras used for beverages.

In the area we call Michigan, the tribes were the Huron, Menominee, Chippewa, Potawatomi, Miami, Kickapoo, Fox and Noquet. Hunting wild animals on the land and fishing comprised the majority of their food sources, as well as wild rice, corn and the mapling of syrup and sugar.

Indiana may have had different Native American tribes, but when the first written records were made, the following were noted in the 1700s: Illini, Shawnee, Miami, Kickapoo, Chippewa, Delaware, Erie and Iroquois. Contrary to modern-day agricultural Indiana, this state was heavily wooded. Therefore, food sources were animals and wild game. The Miami tribe grew a white corn, which was most rare. In order to farm, wooded areas were cleared, and when the soil was depleted, the tribes would relocate to new and fertile land. All tribes traded with other tribes and the Europeans when convenient.

Hasty Pudding, dating to about 1691, is one of the earliest known American desserts. A mixture of milk, cornmeal and molasses, it is also known as Indian Pudding.

"By the end of the 19th century this mush was commercially produced in Chicago and sold in retail stores. Put a pint and a half of milk into a saucepan, add a pinch of salt, and when the milk is just boiling up, sprinkle some fine flour with the left hand and beat well with a fork in the right, to keep the flour from getting lumps. Continue until the pudding is like a stiff, thick batter, which it will be when about a half pound of flour is used. Let is boil 5 or 6 minutes longer, beating it all the time; then turn it into a dish with 2 or 3 ounces of fresh butter and serve immediately. Be sure the milks is quite boiling when the flour is first put in."

(Callahan, Carol. Prairie Avenue Cookbook: Recipes and Recollections from 19th-Century Chicago Families. Carbondale: Southern Illinois University Press, 1993.)

The French

In the mid-1600s, the French came into contact with these peoples. Sweet baking was not a major concern of these early explorers, but they were trying to live off the land as best as they could. When their sugar ran out, they were delighted to "discover" maple sugar and syrup.

Besides expanding the fur trade, the French wanted to find a river passage across North America (for the elusive Northwest Passage to the Far East). They wanted to explore and secure territory and establish their missions to convert the Native Americans to Christianity. The government of Nouvelle-France in Montreal received permission from the Indians in Michigan to let young Frenchmen live among them, learn their languages and customs and become familiar with the landscape and water routes.

The French, however, curious though they were about the native population, were not particularly interested in settling down, colonizing and developing agriculture. One notable exception in Michigan was the planting of fruit trees around Detroit. Three types of apples—Fameuse, Pomme Grise and Red and White Colville—as well as pear trees were planted. The French were quick to learn the ways of the wilderness from the Indians, but they also contributed their sweet traditions. On holidays, the French (both of Minnesota and of Illinois) fed the local Indians.

At first, supplies and people moved into this area from French Canada by way of the St. Lawrence River and the Great Lakes. After New Orleans was founded in 1718, the Mississippi River provided an easier route for trade and exploration.

Wisconsin was more heavily involved with the beaver fur trade through Montreal. Samuel de Champlain had established a fur trading post near Quebec during the 1600s. The Native Americans traded fur for many commodities: metal knives, guns, ammunition and blankets. Fur trading outposts grew along rivers and Lake Michigan.

> *BANNOCK/VOYAGEURS RECIPE*
> *(FRENCH-CANADIAN SETTLERS)*
> *Yield: 6 servings*
>
> *1 cup whole wheat flour*
> *½ teaspoon salt*
> *½ cup flour*
> *2 tablespoons butter, melted*
> *½ cup rolled oats*
> *2 tablespoons sugar, granulated*
> *¾ cup water*
> *about 2 teaspoons baking powder*
>
> *Combine all and bake.*

THE BRITISH

On the other hand, there were the British, the English colonists. Their people steadily advanced westward and overland. They used the waterways when convenient, but their settler mode meant that they were taking over the land. By the eighteenth century, the fur trade had begun to diminish. "In 1760 there had been only 80,000 inhabitants in all of the French North America. By contrast, a decade later, there were, 1,500,000 in the British colonies," according to Clarence Mondale's "The History of the Upper Midwest."

Following the American War of Independence, Britain relinquished territory via the Treaty of Paris (1763), but many fur trappers and traders remained. Michigan, Illinois, Indiana and Wisconsin, also known as a section of the Old Northwest, passed from French to British control.

The Northwest Territory, created by ordinance in 1783, did not just open up new territory south of the Great Lakes, north and west of Ohio and east of the Mississippi. From this date forward, only states were to be admitted to the United States, not just parcels of territories. The Native Americans did not recognize this region as anything but their own. Some of the remaining British stirred up negative feelings between the natives and American frontiersman.

EARLY SWEET BAKING INGREDIENTS

Tribes had different names for corn, but the meaning was the same: "life." Corn was served at most meals in different forms: roasted, boiled and also pounded into flour for breads or a mush-type cereal. Depending on the tribe, season and occasion, fruit and maple syrup and/or sugar might have been incorporated.

Corn cakes without leavening were made in a skillet, a staple for colonists. Johnny cake, or journey cake, was quick and easy to prepare.

Legend has it that it was not just one specific tribe who discovered maple syrup; rather, it was almost universally used by the woodland tribes. One group speaking the Algonquian Native American language called this tree sap "sinzibuckwud," a word for maple syrup (literally, "drawn from wood"). Early French settlers and colonists were shown by the Native Americans how to tap the tree and cook the sap into syrup. Making maple syrup was an enormous task. Thirty-five gallons of sap yielded just one gallon of syrup.

> *JOHNNY CAKE, OR HOE CAKE*
>
> *Scald 1 pint of milk and put in 3 pints of indian meal, and half pint of flower— bake before the fire. Or scald with milk two thirds of the indian meal, or wet two thirds with boiling water, add salt, molasses and shortening, work up with cold water pretty stiff, and bake as above.*
>
> *(Simmons, Amelia. American Cookery. Hartford, CT: printed for Simeon Butler, Northampton, 1798. Reprint, April 14, 2010.)*

Although Christopher Columbus brought the first sugar cane to the Americas from Spain in the late fifteenth century, it was not planted in Louisiana until the early 1700s. Americans wanted sugar, and it was imported in loaf and cone form. Sugar production was so labor-intensive that it became one excuse for beginning slavery. Nevertheless, early sugar farmers were challenged by the weather. While the Caribbean islands offered humid and consistent weather, ideal for sugar cane, the American South chronically encountered freezing temperatures.

Early in America, molasses was the sweetener of choice, due to its affordable price until the 1880s. Molasses was originally imported from the West Indies to distill rum, but the colonists ignored high taxes on sugar cane products. The British lowered the molasses tax in 1764, hoping to gain more compliance.

Turbinado sugar would have been a sugar purchased and used before white granulated sugar due to its lower cost. Turbinado was an early step in the refining process, producing a reliable baking ingredient.

The colonists brought sugar beets to America. No one knows the specific date, but they were well established in the eighteenth century. "George Washington conducted experiments with them at Mount Vernon and by 1888, Burpee's Farm Annual offered twelve varieties of table beets," according to Robert Harveson.

"Sugar Making Among the Indians in the North," nineteenth-century illustration. *Wikimedia Commons.*

Malt extract or malt syrup was and still is used in beer making and in natural ingredient baking today. It is similar to molasses in color and syrup texture. Derived from grains, colonial bakers used it as an alternative sweetener. In fact, the addition of malt was sweeter than cane or beet sugars—its enzymes convert the starches to sugars in baking.

Surprisingly, the Native Americans did not know about honey. The colonists brought bees and plants that depended on pollination in 1622, but honeybees escaped colonists in the East and traveled to the Midwest, contributing to authentic sweet baking there.

Early Flavorings

Salt, of course, is crucial for all baking, sweet or savory. Prized in baking because it strengthens the gluten structure, as well as inhibits yeast growth, a sweet product may only need a pinch. Salt for the colonists came directly from the ocean and was dried in the sun. It was believed that the Onondaga Indians (New York) had done this for five hundred years. Salt played an enormous role in America. When the British attempted to deny the pioneers salt, it served as one motivation to fight and win the Revolutionary War. In fact, the first patent in America authorized by the English Crown was for a particular salt method employed by Edward Winslow of the Massachusetts Bay Colony Company. Winslow was one of the original Pilgrims.

With the Erie Canal, named the "ditch that salt built," the flavoring was a heavy commodity and could be shipped and barged far easier on water as opposed to land. By the time of the Civil War, thousands helped to boil water to extract salt. Eventually, natural rock salt deposits were excavated after the Civil War.

The Pennsylvania Dutch revealed a wide range of spices in the early settlements of William Penn's colony (1680s). In baking and cooking, the spices included cinnamon, ginger, nutmeg, cloves, allspice and cardamom. Cinnamon bun recipes still reign strong in the Philadelphia culinary repertoire today.

Ginger powder was also evident in early colonial recipes. The use of ginger, recorded in ancient Greek history, was part of the English Christmas holiday foods but was not exactly imitated by the colonists, as they shunned Anglican traditions in their new homeland.

Period-Specific Sweet Baked Goods

Gingerbread continued to be a favorite and was no longer just associated with holidays but rather with celebrations as well. "Hard" gingerbreads had traveled with early settlers in various ethnic forms. In Pennsylvania, they were shaped by hand into little pudgy men or Christmas "Mummeli," according to William Weaver.

Before the Civil War, it was mandatory for young men to attend military training in New England. Muster Day, each Tuesday in June, became a festive

---

Amelia Simmons's Coriander Cookies

"One pound of sugar boiled slowly in half pint of water, scum well and cool, add one teaspoon of pearlash, dissolved in milk and then two and a half pounds of flour, rub in four ounces of butter, and two large spoons of finely powdered coriander seed, wet with above; make rolls half and inch thick and cut to the shape you please; bake fifteen or twenty minutes in a flack oven—good three weeks."

(*Simmons, Amelia.* American Cookery.)

occasion, with drink and gingerbread as families celebrated and also attended the military training. "Gemberkoek" of the colonial times is the ginger cake of today. Dutch cookery came to New England and stayed. "Lebkucha" was ginger cake for the Pennsylvania Dutch.

In colonial America, it is difficult to believe that people were already recording recipes, but New England cook Amelia Simmons wrote *American Cookery*. Its repertoire included Independence Cake, Federal Cake and Election Cake. Between 1796 and 1808, four editions were published. The use of spices was already evident.

North America had an abundance of indigenous nut-bearing trees, and Indians of the Midwest frequently gathered walnuts, hickory, pecans and chestnuts for their food. Fur traders brought pecans to the Atlantic coast from Illinois, calling them Illinois nuts, which accounts for the Latin classification of *Illinoinesis*. Pecans come from an Algonquin Indian word, "pacane" ("a nut so hard it had to be cracked with a stone"). Indian tribes believed that the pecan tree was representative of the Great Spirit, and it was used as a major food source during autumn.

European colonists later learned to incorporate many of these nuts into their diets, mainly in the form of baked goods and confections or pressed into oil. The most important of these trees related to the walnut family are the pecan, the butternut, the black walnut and the hickory.

Hernando de Soto, a Spanish explorer, recorded the pawpaw fruit (looking somewhat like a short banana), native to North America in 1540. His writings described how to cultivate the pawpaw, with some plants being sent to Europe in the early 1700s.

Chapter 2

THE AGE OF MANIFEST DESTINY, 1815-1860

NEW TERRITORY

The War of 1812, ending in 1815, is often called the second war of independence from the British. The war was waged for a number of reasons—one, involving the Northwest Territory, was hugely significant. Britain was also involved with the Napoleonic Wars in Europe and thought this "Second American War" to be unimportant.

Each territory in the Northwest Territory could become a state with a population of sixty thousand; Illinois became a state in 1816, followed closely behind by Indiana in 1818. Michigan became a state in 1836 and, much later, Wisconsin in 1848 (the thirtieth state in the union of the United States). "Manifest Destiny is a nineteenth-century belief that the United States had a mission to expand westward across the North American continent, spreading its form of democracy, freedom, and culture," according to the New World Encyclopedia. The expansion was deemed to be not only good but also obvious ("manifest") and certain ("destiny"). Many believed the mission to be divinely inspired, while others felt that it was more an altruistic right to expand the territory of liberty.

The 1849 gold rush sent thousands of people to seek their fortune in California, and it was admitted to the Union the following year with a population of 90,000. West of the Mississippi was now considered the "new" middle west (Midwest). From 1850 to 1860, the Lake Michigan states' populations grew: Indianapolis, from 8,091 to 18,611; Chicago, from 30,000 to 109,000; Milwaukee, from 20,061 to 45,246; and Detroit, from 21,019 to 45,619.

THE IMMIGRANT LANDSCAPE

Immigrants from many lands joined American settlers, who moved westward from the East Coast in the United States in the early 1800s. Frontier life in the Old Northwest (Indian, Illinois, Michigan, Wisconsin, Ohio and parts of Minnesota) was another new terrain for colonists. These people were lured by the inexpensive land and open frontier. Other groups that inhabited the middle states were immigrants seeking religious and political freedom, as well as those seeking jobs, new farmland and more.

In 1790, almost 80 percent of the American population was of British ancestry. The other 20 percent were German, Dutch, Scotch-Irish, French and an assortment of others. By the 1820s, however, larger immigration waves began. Since the new Americans tended to cluster in groups in particular neighborhoods and regions, the middle state farming communities began to emerge as some of the most fertile agricultural areas in the world. Home was a tightknit, relatively homogenous community of Swiss, Dutch, German, Scandinavian or Cornish. These groups, well into the 1830s, dominated the Lake Michigan area. By the 1850s, there were places like Little Switzerland, Wisconsin; Holland, Michigan; Warsaw, Indiana; Shannon, Illinois—authenticity with an American frontier twist. The first Italian immigrants came in the mid-1800s to the Midwest, where sweet baking skills were easily transferable and gave quick opportunities in urban areas, especially Milwaukee and Chicago.

Records indicate that Jews in the Midwest in 1825 were all of English origin, with the exception of a few. They went west, following the path of settlers moving to the Northwest settlement. Jews felt welcome and included in Indiana and, by the 1840s, had established themselves in Fort Wayne, Terre Haute and Lafayette.

The opening of the Erie Canal in 1825 allowed for an easier passage of New Englanders into the Midwest. As each state put land on the market at "low" prices, a strong farm life would spring up, and the immediate cash crops were grains. The Illinois and Michigan Canal—built in 1836 and completed in 1848, predominantly on the sweat of Irish immigrants, thousands of whom had immigrated during the Great Hunger in the 1840s—linked the Great Lakes to the Mississippi and southward to the Gulf of Mexico.

INVENTIONS

Rivers and lakes were natural locations to place water mills and windmills, and once they were built, grain was milled. In 1769, the steamroller mill was invented, and it was no longer necessary to be positioned along waterways. The steamroller increased

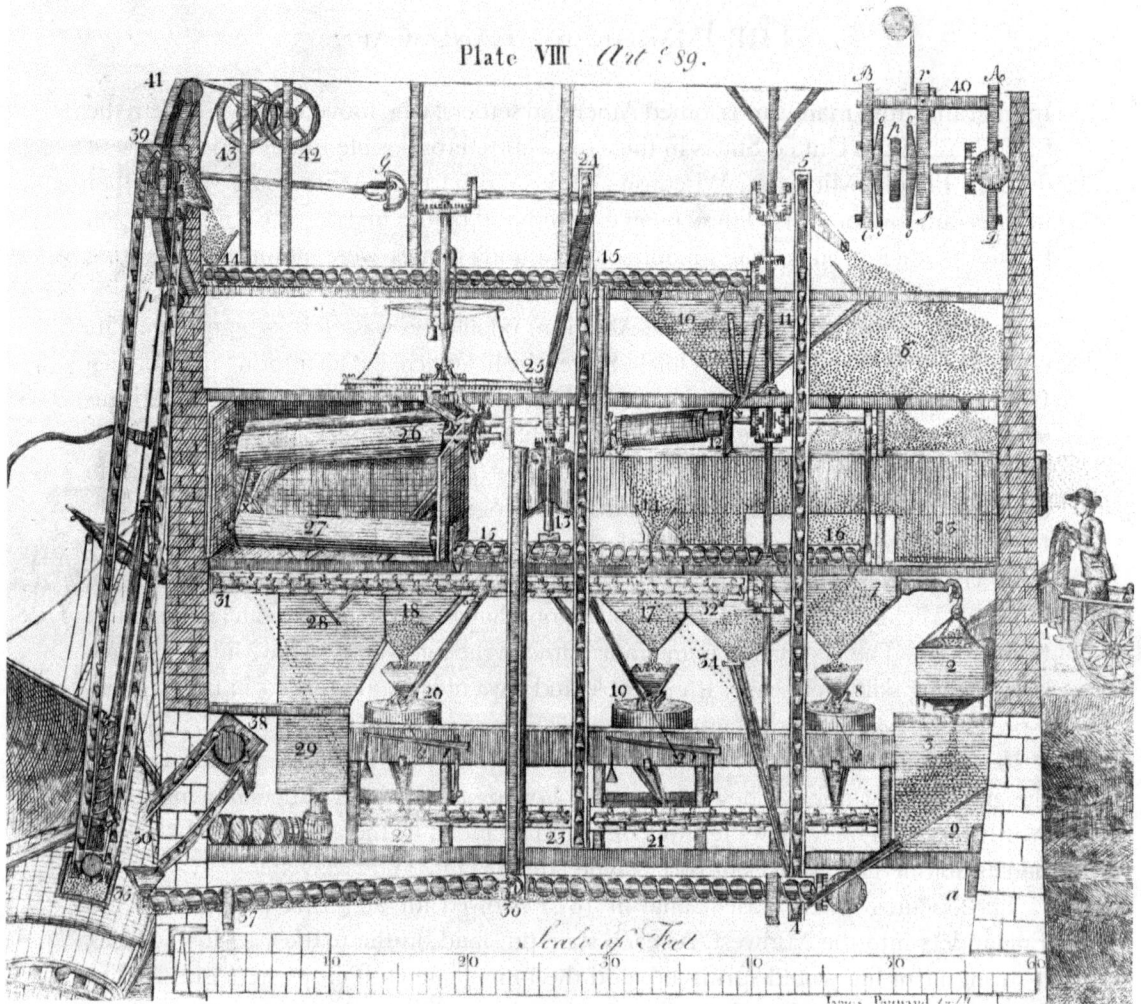

Oliver Evans's design for automated flour milling, 1782. *Wikimedia Commons.*

the capacity of the milling process and also saved grains from turning rancid as they lay in storage bins awaiting production. The automatic mill, grinding grain into flour, was invented by Oliver Evans in Delaware in 1782. What once took four to six men to do soon only took one. Elevators moved grain through various levels of the mill. The milling process was now one continuous system, from cleaning to the final white flour. The mill helped prevent ending up with flour mixed with sawdust and dirt.

Steam-powered flour mills were significant in Chicago during the 1830s, especially for spring wheat. But most grains were never milled locally; rather, they were moved east and processed in Buffalo, New York (along the St. Lawrence seaway), or in Europe, if exported, where it would be freshly milled at the destination.

Illinois congressman Robert Smith leased power rights to flour mills operating along Anthony Falls on the Mississippi River and helped found the Minneapolis Milling Company in 1856. Cadwallader C. Washburn, an attorney and lumber company owner in Wisconsin, purchased the company from Smith. Enormous flour mills were built along the Mississippi, evolving into the present-day company, General Mills, in 1928.

Records indicate that Indianans had almost one thousand mills for grinding their own grain in the middle of the nineteenth century. In 1856, the Igleheart brothers, producer of Swans Down Flour, opened their first flour mill in Evansville, Indiana.

Igleheart Mill, Swans Down Cake Flour, 1890s, The first mill was built in 1856 in Evansville, Indiana. *HistoricEvansville.com.*

STATE FAIRS

In America, dating to the early 1800s, fairs were used as a forum to bring people together. Until the 1920s, most of the population from Indiana, Wisconsin, Illinois and Michigan lived in rural areas. Much of the economy evolved around agriculture. Fairs provided a venue to promote and showcase new products and inventions, as well as entertainment and food. Recipe judging was a category at these fairs. It is here where sweet baking began to demonstrate new ingredients and regional foods. County fair winners would move to the state fair, competing in their respective categories.

INGREDIENTS FOR SWEET BAKING: GRAINS

Colonial settlers had previously lived a life of wheat-based foods. The first settlers brought wheat with them to the colonies but quickly encountered problems with the climate. Humidity in the South and cool climates in the North all but destroyed the crops and the little they had harvested. The colonists would have literally starved were it not for the Native Americans, who introduced them to maize/ corn. Early settlers, nomadic in the early years, without knowledge or the availability of many ingredients, prepared simple fare. Cornmeal plus water and salt resulted in johnny cakes/ journey cakes.

The settlers brought their traditions and foodways with them, and when they could not replicate recipes from their homeland, they used new local ingredients. This mixing and matching yielded the beginnings of the culinary repertoire of the middle states.

It is here where the colonists began to experiment with seeds. They tried to produce stronger, greater-yielding plants. Luckily, the colonists also imported oats, buckwheat and rice. By the 1700s, they

> *INDIAN MEAL PUDDING*
>
> *Rub a tablespoonful of butter round the bottom and sides of a smooth iron kettle—granite or porcelain will do; when melted, add half a cup of boiling water. This will prevent the milk from burning. Add one quart of milk. Let it boil up, and almost over the kettle; then sift in one pint of fine yellow granulated cornmeal, sifting with the left hand, and holding the meal high, that every grain may be thoroughly scalded. Stir constantly; add half a teaspoonful of salt, and set away till cold. Then add half a pint of New Orleans molasses and one quart of cold milk. Put into a well-buttered deep pudding-dish, cover with a plate, and bake very slowly ten or twelve hours. Put it in a "Saturday afternoon oven," where the fire will keep low nearly all night. Let it remain over night, and serve for a Sunday breakfast.*
>
> *(Churchill, Mrs. Barnabas [recipe]. Boston Cooking School Cookbook; Reprint of the 1884 Classic, by Mary J. Lincoln. New York: Dover Publications, 1996. Later republished under Fannie Farmer.)*

were raising successful crops along with corn. Cornbread and johnny cakes became parts of everyday life.

Buckwheat was easily grown and could be harvested within two months. It grew well in poor soil conditions and fit "in between" all of the other growing times for grains. Once considered worthless, it became a stable and reliable grain when farmers were working on the development of new crops.

Learning this new land and understanding what plants would grow to bear fruit and whether one could eat "wild" plants nearby were daily dilemmas. Harsh winters with little fruits and vegetables yielded sick people. Nelson Algren and David E. Schoonover wrote in *America Eats*:

> *Early Illinoisans felt keenly the absence of native fruit. Along toward spring their systems developed a craving for something tart. To satisfy the craving, ingenious housewives invented the vinegar pie—vinegar, molasses, water, a little nutmeg and flour enough to bring the mixture to the consistency of custard. When baked in a pie tin, the resulting product was much relished and remained a favorite springtime dessert until young orchards coming into bearing provided real fruit pies to take its place.*

The English and Dutch who settled in northeastern areas of the United States had brought rye with them. Winter and spring were the only two rye crops. Because rye could grow in poor, sandy soil, it was often relegated to the poorest lands. Indian corn with rye, as well as rye alone, became the ingredients used for bread when wheat crops struggled to yield successful results. Rye was not only used for bread but also for distilling alcohol. ("In 1810 sixty-five distilleries were reported in Hampshire County, Massachusetts," according to Old Sturbridge Village documents.) Two events occurred that affected rye. One was the opening of the Western Canal in New York. Surrounded by more wheat agriculture, that crop took precedence, as it was shipped readily and quickly for consumption. The other factor was the movement of abstinence from alcohol (temperance). Rye was used in many distilleries, further lessening the demand.

Oats, like wheat, were also brought to North America by the early European explorers. The Dutch were responsible for the early plantings in the colonies in 1626. By 1786, George Washington had planted five hundred acres. Mainly grown for animal feed, the Scottish and Dutch mostly used oats in soft foods like porridges and puddings but also in sweet and savory baked goods with names like bannock (a griddlecake that may or may not have a sweetener). Oats, for most Americans, were not used for sweet baking until the late 1800s.

MOLASSES GINGERBREAD

One tablespoon of cinnamon, one spoonful ginger, some coriander or allspice, put to four teaspoons pearlash, dissolved in half pint of water, four pound flour, one quart molasses, six ounces butter (if in winter warm the butter and molasses and pour to the spiced flour), knead well till stiff, the more the better, the lighter and whiter it will be; bake brisk fifteen minutes; don't scorch; before it is put in, wash it with whites and sugar, beat together.

(Simmons, Amelia. American Cookery.)

LEAVENERS

Until the late 1700s, naturally occurring airborne yeast was still the leavening agent of choice. If one waited long enough, yeast spores could naturally land in your flour, or one could place grapes in your flour. Grapes had extra-added yeast spores, increasing the possibility for yeast to settle into the flour. Bread starters, or dough already started by natural fermentation (with the addition of water by the baker), were often kept, and a piece would be pulled off to begin another batch of bread—this was often known as "friendship bread."

Potash/pearlash, impure potassium carbonate, was a product made from the burning of trees into ashes and boiling down the lye with the addition of potassium salts. Potash was used in baking as a leavening agent until the nineteenth century; it also brought cash-short farmers immediate revenue. Nonetheless, a more favored baking soda (sodium carbonate) soon arrived on the scene.

Baking ammonia—a mixture of ammonium carbonate, ammonium bicarbonate and ammonium carbamate (first extracted from the horn/antler of the male deer, thus "hartshorn")—was brought with settlers from western Europe as they began to replicate recipes from their homeland. The ammonia helped a product rise rapidly, needing only heat and moisture.

SWEETENERS

The year of the Louisiana Purchase (1803) reflected a shift in crop planting. Louisiana's plantations shifted from indigo plants to sugar cane. Before the start of the Civil War (1861) Louisiana cane sugar was shipped east in raw form. By the time the United States acquired Puerto Rico and Hawaii, in 1898, the sugar industry was well on its way. Small sugar farms in the South produced cane syrup. As the sugar demand grew, the East Coast imported the raw sugar from the West Indies and began to refine the sugar, eventually producing a dry white sugar.

Brown sugar production was not always one and the same with white sugar. In fact, the brown sugar industry experienced negative exposure when it was claimed that

SPRINGERLE COOKIES

½ teaspoon baker's ammonia (hartshorn)
2 tablespoons water
6 large eggs, room temperature
6 cups sifted powdered sugar
½ cup softened unsalted butter (a little more or less is okay)
½ teaspoon salt
½ teaspoon flavor of your choice (more if desired)
8 cups sifted cake flour
more flour as needed

Dissolve hartshorn in water and set aside. Beat eggs till thick and lemon-colored (10–20 minutes). Slowly beat in the powdered sugar, then the softened butter.

Add the hartshorn and water, salt, preferred flavoring, and grated rind of lemon, lime or orange, if using. Let this mixture mix on medium speed for about 30 minutes or so. At times if I'm busy I let it beat for 40 minutes or more. Gradually beat in as much flour as you can with the mixer. Turn onto floured surface and knead in enough of the remaining flour to make a good print with the springerle mold, without sticking.

DRYING

After trimming your Springerle allow them to dry for between 16–24 hours before baking. This will allow the image from the mold to crust and thus prevent it from being distorted. Large Springerle can take from 24–48 hours to dry. Bake on baker's parchment-lined cookie sheets at 225° to 300° till barely golden on the bottom, 15–30 minutes or more, depending on size of cookie. Store in airtight containers. Yield: 3 to 12 dozen.

[Springerle literally translates in old German dialect, "little knight" or "jumping horse." Julfest, a pagan midwinter celebration, called for celebratory foods. Thus the origin of this cookie made with a wooden mold, imprinted with varying images. Contemporary rolling pins with cut-outs on the entire pin are used for modern day production.]

(Current Captivating Copper Country Cooking. Compiled by a First Presbyterian Church Circle in Houghton, Michigan. Calumet, MI: Keewenah Printing Company, 1930s.)

dirty microbes were in the brown sugar. Recipes from about the 1900s proclaim brown sugar to be inferior and loaded with bugs.

The beet sugar industry was slow to grow due to the hand labor necessary for farming. Sugar beets grew in areas where slaves were not necessarily available. Numerous attempts were made to introduce beet production in the 1830s, 1840s and 1850s, but most factories just closed.

SORGHUM COOKIES

1 cup butter	½ cup sugar
3½ cups flour	1 teaspoon powdered ginger
1 cup sorghum	2 eggs beaten
1 teaspoon baking soda	1 teaspoon salt

Place first three ingredients in a saucepan and heat until melted, stirring frequently. Let cool to lukewarm. Add eggs and beat mixture. In a separate bowl sift together flour, soda, ginger and salt.
   Gradually stir dry ingredients into egg mixture. Chill dough. Roll out and cut into shapes. Bake on greased cookie sheets in 350 F. oven 18–20 minutes.

(Old Brown County Receipts. Nashville, IN: Bear Wallow Books, 1983.)

EGG CUSTARD PIE RECIPE

Speculation and folklore has it that Angel Food Cake could have originated with the Pennsylvania Dutch. Great noodle makers, they may have taken the extra egg whites and prepared new recipes.

4 eggs	1 teaspoon vanilla
2 cups milk	nutmeg
1 cup sugar	

Stir eggs, milk, sugar and vanilla until well blended. Pour into pie shell, sprinkle generously with nutmeg and bake at 350 for 45–50 minutes or until set.

Sorghum, as another available sweetener, grew as a tall grass stalk. In late fall, harvest occurred and families gathered to help one another; they cut them into strips and hitched a horse to a small cider press. The sap was squeezed into a barrel and cooked over a fire until golden brown.

EGG METHODS

Early Midwest settlers brought chickens with them as they migrated to their destinations, thus ensuring the availability of eggs. As the middle states industrialized, eggs were readily available from a grocer or farmer delivering eggs to the city.

MILK AND MILK PRODUCT METHODS

Cheese making has been around since early history. Stories relay cheese being accidentally made by the storage of goat milk in a goat stomach or portable bag. The milk changed into cheese curds. Early goat herders began to wonder if something inside this stomach bag could have something to do with the milk changing. Natural rennet (acid) in the stomach bag changed the fresh milk to curds.
   Early cheese making was labor- and time-intensive. Immigrants brought with them the methods and techniques to make their specialty cheeses in America. Puritan women were the cheese makers from the seventeenth to the nineteenth century. "Soft" cheeses used in sweet baking—ricotta, Baker's cheese and mascarpone—were easy to make on a small batch basis. Many cheese-making

methods for sweet baking were brought by Italian immigrants to the new frontier, especially the ricotta- and mascarpone-style cheeses.

Cream cheese, as a sweet baking ingredient, may have existed, but it was not recognized with this name.

BUTTER

Until the nineteenth century, most butter was prepared by hand on farms. The all-purpose family cow pulled the plow, provided milk for various dairy products and eventually became butchered meat. Different churning apparatus for butter were available, from the traditional wooden barrel with the long stick to the small glass bottle and crank handle for the home.

EARLY THICKENING METHODS

Early sweet baking was simplistic. The early settlers prepared products without access to numerous ingredients. The most logical and natural thickener for sweets would be reductions. In other words, if you were baking a fruit pie, you would heat and reduce down the fruit juices, not only thickening the juice but also concentrating the flavors. Of course, adding sugar to a mixture and cooking it over the fire also thickened the product. The sugar crystals, when cooked, turned into a liquid and then began to thicken the mixture.

The addition of flour could also thicken a recipe. Classic European sauces from the sixteenth century used flour (a roux, butter and flour cooked, and also beurre monie, a mixture of flour and butter, chilled, rolled and stirred into a sauce) to thicken a savory sauce. When cooks realized that this same flour had the possibility of thickening a sweet custard sauce, flour was, alas, used for this purpose as well. These European traditions were carried to the Midwest as immigrants traveled. Coating fruits with flour also kept the natural juices in the mixture while helping the baker keep the crust from becoming soggy.

A RICH CAKE RECIPE

Take six pounds of the best fresh butter, work it to a cream with your hands; then throw in by degrees three pounds of double refined sugar well beat and sifted; Mix them well together; then work in three pounds of blanched almonds, and having them altogether till they are thick and look white. Then add half a pint of French brandy, half a pint of sack, a small quantity of ginger, about two ounces of mace, cloves, and cinnamon each, and three large nutmegs all beaten in a mortar as fine as possible. Then shake in gradually four pounds of well dried and sifted flour; and when the oven is well prepared, and a thin hoop to bake it in, stir into this mixture (as you put it into the hoop) seven pounds of currants clean washed and rubbed, and such a quantity of candied orange, lemon, and citron in equal proportions, as shall be thought convenient. The oven must be quick, and the cake at least will take four hours to bake; Or you may make two or more cakes out of these ingredients, you must beat it with your hands, and the currants must be dried before the fire, and put into the cake warm.

(Carter, Susannah. The Frugal Colonial Housewife. *N.p., 1772. Reprinted in America by Benjamin Edes and John Gil.)*

NUTS IN EARLY SWEET BAKING

Nut cakes and nut breads have been parts of American baking from early to contemporary recipes. English settlers began planting pecan trees in the 1700s, realizing the economic potential for this nut. The commercial propagation of pecans began in the 1880s.

According to *American Food: The Gastronomic Story*, pioneers from the East Coast adapted pumpkin pies by adding black walnuts, as well as adding those nuts to cakes, cookies and frostings. "Throughout the Middle West especially—lavish black walnut cakes are perennial favorites. Black John Cake is of two layers made from dough that blends brown sugar, molasses, eggs, butter, flour, ginger, cinnamon, buttermilk, and baking soda and has a filling accented by raisins, coconut, and black walnuts."

MARY TODD LINCOLN CAKE

President Lincoln's wife, Mary Todd Lincoln, made a vanilla almond cake for him while they were courting in Springfield, Illinois, in the 1840s, as well as during their time in the White House, 1861–65. This particular recipe has been updated to reflect modern times.

INGREDIENTS

1 cup almonds

1 cup butter

1½ cups sugar

2¼ cups all-purpose flour

1 tablespoon baking powder

1⅓ cups milk

6 egg whites

1 teaspoon vanilla extract

confectioners' sugar

INSTRUCTIONS

Preheat the oven to 375F. Grease and flour two 9-inch round layer cake pans or one Bundt cake pan. Use a food processor to grind the almonds into a course flour. Cream the butter and sugar to mix them until fluffy. Sift the flour and baking powder to mix them together, then fold the dry flour mix into the creamed butter and sugar, alternating with milk, until well blended. Stir in the almond powder and mix thoroughly.

In a separate bowl, beat the egg whites until they form stiff peaks. Add a pinch of salt for easier stiffening. Add vanilla extract. Gently fold the egg whites into the batter with a rubber spatula. Pour the batter into the pan(s) and bake for 30 minutes or until a toothpick inserted into the center comes out clean. Cool for at least 15 minutes before flipping the cake out of the pan, and allow it to completely cool before serving. If a layer cake was made, use a jam for filling. Sift confectioners' sugar on top for decoration.

FRUITS IN EARLY SWEET BAKING

Cranberry farming began in the 1800s, with the first growers picking the cranberries by hand. Eventually, more developed harvesting techniques were acquired, and then a revolutionary idea called wet harvesting was developed. Cranberries are grown in sandy bogs and marshes, and in wet harvesting, the fields are flooded when the fruit is ready for harvesting, giving the impression that cranberries grow in water. The cranberries can then be easily scooped up. Wisconsin's first harvest was in 1860.

According to Michigan history, "In 1865 there were 207,639 peach trees in and around St. Joseph and Benton Harbor. There also were approximately 70,000 apple, 40,000 pear, 10,000 cherry, 2,500 quince and 3,000 plum trees, as well as 'more strawberry, blackberry, and raspberry plants than could be enumerated.' But the peach was king," according to William Armstrong.

Apples, a predominant fruit grown in Michigan, Illinois, Indiana and Wisconsin, were never indigenous to the area. Remember, the French planted a few types in the 1700s in the Detroit area, but the Pilgrims brought seeds to colonial America, and as settlers moved west, the seeds moved with them. Johnny Appleseed, a true legend, is also responsible for planting apple seeds as he traveled the middle states.

"Such is the remarkable story of Johnny Appleseed, which has been frequently repeated, but may bear retelling in the light of recent developments. The important thing to notice is that he carried out a large tree-planting project single-handed. Far ahead of the government, he saw the need for more trees, and while he was about it, he planted trees that would supply food. In inaugurating vast schemes for reforestation and drought control, the government is only following in his footsteps."

"Old sower, Johnny Appleseed,
Now sow into a rhyme thy creed."
When the corn you plant,
Be not of seed too scant;
If the field you would rightly till,
Put-in four grains to the hill;
One for the mouse and one for the crow,
One to rot and one to grow;
Then shall the tiller,
Surely see the miller.

("Full Text of 'Johnny Appleseed's Rhymes.'")

FLAVORINGS

Calvin Sawyer arrived from Ohio in St. Joseph County, Michigan, in 1835, planting the first peppermint in the soil. Peppermint (*Mentha piperita*) and spearmint (*Mentha spicata*) are said to have originated in the Mediterranean. These flavors began to be used as ingredients in sweet baking, foods, medicines and fragrances. By the end of the Civil War in 1865, Michigan supplied 90 percent of the world's mint oil.

PERIOD-SPECIFIC SWEET BAKED GOODS

The settlers brought their traditions and foodways with them, and when they could not replicate recipes from their homeland, they used new local ingredients. Indigenous fruits—pawpaw and persimmon—might have replaced pears and plums; corn and buckwheat would suffice for wheat. This mixing and matching yielded the new culinary repertoire of the middle states.

At first, some middle states had sweet specialties specific to the local ingredients. Indiana settlers found amber-colored fruit growing wild (persimmon) that had a sweet pulp and, when combined with varying ingredients, prepared delicious sweet puddings and breads. Settlers in these new middle states began to create a new identity.

The late 1800s saw eastern Europeans bringing hearty everyday fare to most of the Lake Michigan states. Czechs, Hungarians, Poles and Bohemians yielded butter cookies, Kolachke (yeast pastries filled with fruit jelly), strudel and Paczki (doughnuts filled with jelly or custard), as well as Milosti (fried dough with powdered sugar, Czech in origin). Braetzli, rolled cookies (Swiss origins) and Danish kringles (a pastry dough filled with fruits and or nuts, covered with icing), its distinct oval shape still making it unique today, were also favorites. Brown Betties (baked fruits with buttered crumbs), brought with the colonists moving west, became cobblers (baked fruit with dollops of biscuit on top) and crisps (crumbs made from crackers, flour, nuts and mixture). These sweet baked items were simple and easy to prepare, with ingredients that might have been in one's pantry or were easily purchased through bartering or by using money in stores.

Bannock to the Scots, scones to the Irish and Welsh and cakes to those originating from Wales—all were "quick breads," made with simple ingredients like flour, sour milk/milk/buttermilk, butter, sultanas/currants/raisins, baking soda or powder and a scant amount of salt and sugar. The dried fruit used might indicate where you lived. Raisins were most likely from America because currants were from Europe. Small round "scone" shapes were individual servings, and large round shapes were cut into slices. These baked easily in a hearth fire and might be accompanied by jelly or jam.

OLD FASHIONED STEAMED PERSIMMON LOAF

1 cup yellow stone ground cornmeal
1 teaspoon salt
1 cup rye flour
1 cup sour milk
1 cup whole wheat
1 cup persimmon pulp
2 teaspoons baking soda
¾ cup molasses
1 cup chopped raisins

Combine cornmeal, flours, soda and salt. In a separate bowl combine buttermilk, pulp, molasses, and raisins. Add batter to dry ingredients. Mix well. Pour into 2 buttered 1-quart pudding molds or 2 1-pound buttered coffee cans. Butter lids before closing molds and tie lids on. Steam 3 hours in 1 inch of water.

(Old Fashioned Persimmon Recipes. "Persimmon Breads." Indiana: Bear Wallow Books, 2004.)

HODGSON MILL: BOB AND CATHY GOLDSTEIN

Illinois is a long state, 390 miles long, and Effingham, Illinois, is about 200 miles from Chicago and also where my trip began. Effingham is where Hodgson Mill is located. I arrived at a busy, modern-equipped town (with hotels, restaurants and shops) looking for a "little mill." Surrounded by farmland interspersed with the railroad and highway, I did not expect to really find a small mill but was surprised to see an operation with wind turbines and solar panels. Yet the stones grinding grains are still the same type as when Hodgson Mill first began.

Hodgson Mill's water wheel–powered grain mill, 1897. *Hodgson Mill.*

BUCKWHEAT-CORN MUFFINS
(HODGSON MILL RECIPE COLLECTION)

1 cup Hodgson Mill Buckwheat Flour
½ cup Hodgson Mill Yellow Cornmeal
2 ½ teaspoons baking powder
½ teaspoon salt
¼ cup sugar
2 eggs, beaten
1 ¼ cups milk
¼ cup melted butter

Preheat oven to 400 F. Line 12 muffin cups with paper liners or grease muffin cups. Mix together buckwheat flour, cornmeal, baking powder, salt and sugar. Combine eggs, milk and butter; beat. Add to dry ingredients; stir just until dry ingredients are moistened (batter will be thin). Fill muffin tins ⅔ full. Bake 15–20 minutes or until done. Yield: 12 muffins.

The renewable energy systems installed at the mill headquarters consist of four solar panels and two high-efficiency wind turbines. They produce enough energy to power the entire sales and marketing office. Hodgson has a *Whole Grain Baking* cookbook that reflects many midwestern recipes. The book's recipes range from coffeecakes to doughnuts, as well as cookies and scones. All Hodgson products have recipes on the exterior of the packaging that reflect the midwestern palate.

Mr. Ray Martin, sales and marketing manager, for Hodgson, arranged a tour of the mill, where many friendly locals work. Touring a food production plant always requires a coat and hairnet, but here extra precautions were taken for the gluten-free area. Wiping shoes and wearing an apron, only in this area, were just a few extra steps to ensure that the specific "gluten-free" area remained uncontaminated.

The staff explained the new standards toward which their facility is working: certification by the British Retail Consortium. This global product safety and quality certification will be another way Hodgson can ensure that customers a "true quality product." After touring the facility and meeting staff throughout, the president and owner, Mr. Bob Goldstein, joined us. Both Bob and his wife, Cathy, live near the mill. Bob grew up on a large farm and has his roots in milling, while Cathy is a fifth-generation miller. Most friendly, Bob greeted us dressed in a cowboy hat, boots and vest.

Bob and Cathy Goldstein, Hodgson Mills, Effingham, Illinois

Q. What is the "story" behind Hodgson Mill?
A. Hodgson Mill was born from the legacy of Alva Hodgson, a pioneering Missouri millwright, and the sturdy, water-driven grain mill that came to bear his name. Found deep in the rugged heart of the Missouri Ozarks, the original mill site was already being used by 1837. A second mill, built in 1861, burned down as Missouri passed through the chaos of the Civil War. The mill used on our packaging was completed in 1897 and operated into the 1960s and was started up again in 1970. Since 2004, the facility has been located in Effingham, Illinois. The current location utilizes the area for ease of transport to our customers.

Q. Is the mill the same as it always has been since the founding?
A. The milling stone equipment has been the same (using red granite from North Carolina); the source for energy has changed. In 2009, a change occurred as Hodgson Mill had always been proud of their commitment to the environment; this move to use renewable, natural sources of power to make our all natural and organic products, really reaffirms our core mission.

Q. What differs today in milling as compared to one hundred years ago?
A. Competition! Getting your product on the shelf and known to the consumer.

Q. Do you know the people who grow the grain you are milling?
A. We need to have strong relationships with our suppliers. For example, we are going through the process of ensuring that our products are verified as Non-GMO. Another way of saying that is that we expect that the grains we use are grown from seeds that are not genetically modified. That means that through our suppliers, relationships have to be built clear back to the farmers and the type of seed they use. Sixty-six of our products verified Non-GMO [Genetically Modified Organisms], *and more will be verified soon. We also do not allow the use of BHTs* [butylated hydroxytoluene], *which is a preservative used to keep grains from becoming rancid. To ensure that we are giving and providing our consumers the highest-quality natural products, strong, trusting relationships with a specific number of suppliers is a must.*

Q. Have your customers changed over the years?
A. When Alva Hodgson was selling flours and meals, it was directly to the local population. It was truly a Midwest brand. We now market to the entire country. We do, however, try to preserve the Midwest values in the way we go about our business.

Q. Do you observe any new trends or changes in sweet baking in the Midwest?

A. In recent years, consumers have become increasingly more health- and nutrition-conscious and have begun to recognize the importance of grain-based foods in their diets. Also, gluten-free requests are very important.

Q. What makes your company unique as compared to other mills in the Midwest and/or the country?

A. The way Hodgson Mill grinds grains today is not much different from the way it was back in 1882. We still mill the grain with stones, in a classic, time-honored way. This immediate use of the milled grains gives our customer the freshest possible products. Hodgson Mill's products are considered premium quality because of the top-notch grains we use, as well as our special stone milling techniques. Each of our five stone mills produces only about eight hundred pounds of whole grain product an hour. That's not a lot when compared to large flour companies. Pasta is also produced using whole wheat, organic grain and gluten-free ingredients.

Q. Would you like to share other information or stories?

A. The previous owner of Hodgson in the 1970s was blending flours pretty much by the barrel. Driving it into possible customers. Waiting to see who might be interested… well the day came, a big day. The grocer Kroger said they would take a truck full. Well, Ken Harrington said he would drive his pickup truck to the grocer. No, the grocer meant they would be there with a semi truck ready to pick it up. This is a sign of "making it big." Very Big!

Chapter 3

MIDDLE STATE CHANGES, 1860-1900

CHANGES

What was happening to the population and culture in the Lake Michigan states at the time of the Civil War and after? Europe's poor economy and failing conditions drove people out, while freedom, opportunity for land and jobs lured immigrants to America. By 1880, 15 million immigrants had made their way to the United States, many choosing agriculture in the Midwest and Northeast.

The Lake Michigan territory was no longer the new rural frontier, but it was dotted with population centers on their way to becoming great cities. The Midwest, with its abundant natural resources, gave birth to Detroit, Chicago, Milwaukee and Indianapolis, not to mention innumerable other smaller gathering spots like Fort Wayne, St. Joseph and Springfield. The concentration of ethnic populations that had filled the farming countryside now filled blocks and blocks of new city enclaves.

This concentration of ethnic groups in cities meant that traditions would be intensified in many a Little Italy or Greektown, as well as in Polish and Swedish neighborhoods, where the languages of Europe held sway for generations—and where languages flourished, so also did food traditions and recipes. Ethnic density spurred the new Americans to hold on to their old traditions. These enclaves guaranteed that the American sweet palate would necessarily include flavors from many lands. The cities may have been melting pots in the workplace, but neighborhoods and small towns held fast to the traditions and foodways of old. While two factory workers might both solder wheels on the job, they would sit down to lunch, each with his own lunch bucket, and out would come a German cake, a Polish sweet or an Italian biscotti.

Perhaps they might trade sweets, and one of them might bring home an extra piece of the other man's lunch to share with his wife. The result was an expansion of foods, not a merging, and both new Americans were richer for it.

The Scripture Cake recipe here has origins with groups that emigrated from Europe, landing in Michigan's upper peninsula.

Don't be fooled by all of the handmade bakery items; cookie, biscuit and cracker makers were forming a group of more than one hundred bakeries. When united, the National Biscuit Company and American Biscuit and Manufacturing emerged. It called itself the National Biscuit Company in 1898 (Nabisco), marketing and manufacturing cookies and biscuits from headquarters in Chicago. Biscuits are what we call crackers in the United States. German bakers in Chicago became the first to unionize and formalize baking employees.

SCRIPTURE CAKE

1 cup butter (Judges 5:25)
3½ cups flour (1 Kings 4:22)
1 cup sugar—½ brown and ½ granulated (Jeremiah 6:20)
2 cups raisins (1 Samuel 30:12)
2 cups figs (1 Samuel 30:12)
1 cup water (Genesis 24:17)
1 cup almonds (cut) (Genesis 43:11)
6 eggs (Isaiah 10:14)
a little salt (Leviticus 2:13)
1 tablespoon honey (Exodus 16:31)
spices to taste (1 Kings 10:10)

Follow Solomon's advice for making good boys and you will have a good cake. Proverbs 23:14

With weights and measures just and true
Oven of even heat;
Well buttered tins, and quiet nerves,
Success will be complete

(Current Captivating Copper Country Cooking.)

CIVIL WAR IMPACT

Most significant in this period was the Civil War (1861–65). European immigrants joined the Union army in large numbers, including 177,000 born in Germany and 150,000 born in Ireland. Many Germans saw the parallel between slavery and serfdom in the old fatherland, and the Irish, speaking English and escaping crowded cities, saw a road to advancement in the military. The war went on for four years, taxing the Union's capacity to supply its army and forcing the development of mass production of foods and transportation methods. The McCormick reaper increased grain production enough to feed the North and its armies, as well as export grain to help finance the war.

One example of a specific food that served the military's needs was canned milk. The first canned milk, allowing for no risk of perishability, came from Borden. Later, an employee would begin his own canned milk company in Illinois: PET Milk. "Yankees crossing their thresholds once more got the oysters they had done without, and the home baked pies that could not keep up with their advancing armies during the war," according to William Davis's *A Taste for War.*

Perhaps the largest impact of the Civil War was a sense of "coming together." The immigrants fought as Americans, side by side, regardless of the land from which their parents came. The unity held, and Americans became one people. Most soldiers wanted a taste of their "traditional" family foods, including sweet baked goods. Home is always home. But they now knew of other kinds of people, and their curiosity enabled exploration of other cuisines recognizable in other cities and neighborhoods.

More rural general stores sprung up after the Civil War; you could barter or pay cash for coffee, salt and sugar. The corner store and bakery typically served homogenous communities, but this began to change, especially in locations where one bakery served increasingly mixed communities. Women, classically the shoppers, might encounter unfamiliar food products. The Jewish needs and the Swedish and German tastes would be met by one shop. Certainly, there were narrowly focused ethnic stores, but inevitably more products became available to more people. Tastes expanded. The Irish Scots wanted a Kolachke, and Germans began to like soda bread.

CHALLENGING FOOD

Bakery signs with familial names often indicated the presence of ethnic groups residing nearby, as well as expected sweet baked offerings. Chicago's records indicated that "according to the 'Census of Manufacturers of 1850's there are 2,027 bakeries in the United States."

But American women also baked far more at home compared to Europeans. Baking fuel was more readily available and affordable. Reliable roads, railroads and, eventually, the truck and automobile dramatically changed the landscape of the Lake Michigan states by the 1900s. Industrialization meant that jobs were open to those who previously had looked for a future on the farm. A rapid concentration of people now converged on urban centers. But this concentration brought with it complex problems of food management and distribution in the new cities. Eggs, milk, flour and other baking ingredients all had to be purchased.

The cities grew so fast that there were no systems of food distribution or food safety. Milk, which was used in sweet baking, used to come from the cows in the barn or, on the outskirts of the cities, from the milk cow in a "garage." But in the teeming inner-city tenements, supplies of milk were so scarce and adulterated that many residents gave their children beer rather than risk illness from polluted milk. Baking with tainted milk yielded unsatisfactory and even dangerous results. Dealers often skimmed off all the cream to make butter and then further thinned the skim milk with water. To thicken the product after the removal of the cream, unscrupulous dealers used chalk dust, borax and plaster.

The first dairy inspections in the country began in Chicago in 1867. Tainted milk was regarded as a central cause of the alarming death rate among children. Physicians began to prescribe condensed milk for children. Greater demand for this milk meant greater production, and more sweet recipes began using these "new canned" milk production. Food reform became the watchword in the late 1800s. By 1900, regulations and inspections were in place that did away with most of these abuses, but the impact on sweet baking had been costly. "Waves of anger met each revelation [about] adulteration, unclean preparation and sale conditions. There were chemicals in tea, condiments, vinegar, cider, nuts, soda pop, ice cream, candy maple sugar, honey, baked goods, and breakfast cereal," according to Perry Duis's "Food" in *Challenging Chicago, Coping with Everyday Life*.

POPULATION CHANGE

An 1850 census tells us that 90 percent of the nation were native born. Movements of people from south to north occurred, especially after the Civil War. A rise in immigration contributed to a greater mix of populations; shifting populations also occurred due to the young men lost in the Civil War. During this period, the largest population group to arrive in America was from German-speaking regions in Europe. Germans settled in all four of the Lake Michigan states.

The 1880s saw the strongest Scandinavian immigration in Wisconsin. Dairy was a part of their traditions. Illinois also had a strong Swedish population, though at the turn of the century in 1900. New spices found their way into these baked goods: caraway, cardamom, cinnamon and anise seeds. As they moved west, Moravians from Bohemia, French Huguenots and German brethren brought with them spices from European stock and recipe traditions, like rich butter kringle coffeecake and spritz-style cookies. Doughnuts found their way into the culinary palate via the Dutch settlers in New Amsterdam (New York) as olykoeks, meaning "oily cakes." "The first doughnuts had no holes. They were small 'nuts' of dough. Fried in lard and eventually oil. Holes were commonly cut into the center...using an available round utensil—perhaps a sewing thimbles, which made the confection convenient for dunking into coffee. Doughnut cutters soon followed, appearing in catalogs by the 1890s," according to Carol Callahan's *Prairie Avenue Cookbook*.

The two most populous centers with German descent in 1900 were Wisconsin (34 percent of its population) and Illinois' Chicago (25 percent of the population). Before long, there were German-language cookbooks being printed in Wisconsin. The most prominent of these was Henriette Davidis's *Praktiches Kochbuck fur die Deutshen in Amerika*, 1879. Reflecting the importance of bread and cake in German food and culture, there was a special section on baking. German traditions of "Kaffee und Teegesellshaften" (coffee and tea) parties were also included. Eighteen years later, in the second edition, measurements became Anglicized and recipes began changing, "Maisbrot/cornbread" as an example.

Acculturation was happening. Native languages were still spoken at home, enough where we see cookbooks still printed in non-English languages, but the food traditions and way of life were already giving way to the dominant new American culture.

INVENTIONS

The McCormick reaper, introduced in 1834, reduced the manpower from five people to only two people in the fields. The McCormick disk plow of 1847 planted rows evenly for farmers with cereal grains. Combine harvesters were introduced in the 1890s; with the addition of the internal combustion engine, the entire seed-to-harvest cycle could be done on hundreds of acres! The varying grains could be harvested and baled, first pulled by horses and then later mechanized.

> These little individual pies were used for miner's meals, and were often reheated on a shovel over the candle the miner wore on his hat. They were filled with hand-chopped meat (suet), onions, potatoes, carrots or rutabagas, and sometimes an all-in-one-meal had a fruit filler (cherries, peaches, apples) in one end.
>
> (McKee, Gwen, and Barbara Moseley. "Meats" Best of the Best From Michigan. Mississippi: Quail Ridge Press, 1996.)

The next question was how to get the grain to market. Locations without water transportation were at a big disadvantage. By the time of the Civil War, railroads had been built, and agricultural products went by rail. After the "wheat frontier" had passed through an area, more diversified farms, including those for dairy cattle, generally took its place. Slave labor was used in the South until after the Civil War, especially for the labor-intensive farming of sugar, tobacco and cotton. The Freedom Ordinance of 1787, long before the Civil War ended in 1865, prohibited slavery in the new middle states. No slavery for crop production was a disadvantage for profits to farmers as compared to the South.

In 1877, Washburn Mills partnered with Crosby and formed the Washburn-Crosby Company. Enormous flour mills were built along the Mississippi River, and old grinding stones were replaced with automatic steel rollers. In 1928, the company acquired twenty-six more mills and was renamed General Mills.

Large flour mills became centralized in large cities in about the 1900s, and rural mills slowly began to close. Mid-century, Henry Jones innovated self-rising flour, and U.S. mills began to follow suit (flour plus baking powder and salt, resulting in self-rising flour).

Northern Wisconsin and the upper Michigan territories had a timber culture. Vast trees and mining for ore attracted Cornish miners first, as well as Swedish, Finnish and, later, Croatians and Slovenes. The miners carried pastry pies, known as pasties, into the caves. Stories told by the "uppers" (Upper Michigan people) relay how the miners' wives put initials into the pastry crust so that the pies would not get mixed up when eating. The crust protected the filling from arsenics used in the mine below.

The first simple icebox, with an ice compartment below, was developed in about 1803. Icemen delivered blocks of ice to homes and businesses. Mechanized refrigeration in 1834, along with the ice blocks, ensured food preservation. Food was not only refrigerated at home but now also by rail car and ships. Perishables could be moved and shipped from ports inland, and Lake Michigan state products could be shipped outbound.

Glass jars were first used for commercial and home food preservation, but by the 1850s, competition in the metal canning industry yielded shelf-stable canned products in most Americans homes.

Open hearths and brick ovens were the norm until this time. Enclosed wood-burning stoves with flues or dampers helped regulate heat and gave more precise cooking temperatures. By the late 1800s, home bakers were further spurred by several innovations. The cast-iron kitchen stove, complete with its own quickly heated oven, became standard equipment in urban middle-class homes.

Michigan Stove, located in Detroit, Michigan, had a strong reputation for its equipment, but by the close of the nineteenth century, its notoriety had soared. At

> ### PASTIES
>
> #### PASTRY
> 3 cups flour
> 1 teaspoon salt
> 1 cup lard
> ½ cup cold water
>
> #### FILLING
> 1½ pounds beef
> 3 medium potatoes
> ½ pound pork steak and some suet
> 2 onions
> 2 rutabaga
>
> Divide pastry into 6 parts. Roll into size of plate. Place filling over half, prick dough on upper half. Fold over, crimp, bake at 325 F. for 1 hour. Add fruit jelly inside if desired.
>
> (MRS. LEWIS, HUBBELL, MICHIGAN)

the World's Columbian Exposition in Chicago in 1893, owner and founder Jeremiah Dwyer built an enormous stove for its exhibit. Millions of people saw this fifteen-foot-high stove weighing fifteen tons. Michigan Stove also built commercial stoves using the name Garland.

Kitchens had been around for centuries, but many small appliance inventions occurred around this time. Most households did not have servants, and women spent time working alone and needed culinary help: vegetable and fruit peelers, dicers and mashers and even a wooden dishwasher. The most significant kitchen inventions, those using electricity, were created at the turn of the century.

Small kitchenware—like rolling pins, pie pans and cake pans—had always been important in the production of sweet baked products. There were numerous companies manufacturing baking equipment around the Lake Michigan states for both commercial and home bakers. One manufacturer, Austrian-born Edward Katzinger, manufactured tin pans for bakeries in Chicago. Baking ingredient companies soon looked to these manufacturers to emboss their names on equipment, to literally "brand" the company name into baker's minds.

During the late 1800s, cookbooks were beginning to explain the "proper" way to use an oven. Books about cooking arrived in the 1840s, but before this, many recipes were passed on orally using rhymes, as not all people were literate. A most impressionable and important book for baking was Fannie Merritt Farmer's 1896 work in which she replaced terms such as "handful" "pinch" and "sprinkle" with exact measurements.

Noted Fannie Farmer: "A cooking-stove is a large iron box on legs. It has a fire-box in the front, the sides of which are lined with fire-proof material similar to that of which bricks are made. The bottom is furnished with a movable iron grate. Underneath the fire-box is a space which extends from the grate to a pan for receiving ashes. At the back of fire-box is a compartment called the oven, accessible on each side of the stove by a door. Between the oven and the top of the stove is a space for the circulation of air."

RYE GEMS

1⅔ cups rye flour

¼ cup molasses

1⅓ cups flour

1¼ cups milk

4 teaspoons baking powder

2 eggs

1 teaspoon salt

3 tablespoons melted butter

Mix and sift dry ingredients, add molasses, milk, eggs well beaten, and butter. Bake in hot oven in buttered gem pans for twenty-five minutes.

(Farmer, Fannie. The Original Fannie Farmer 1896 Cookbook. *Italy: Ottenheimer Publishers, 1996.*)

STATE FAIRS

The first state fair in the United States was held in Detroit, Michigan, in 1849. State fairs were important gatherings for early inhabitants. Many in the population lived in rural areas, and this event allowed participants and attendees to share, learn and formulate new ideas. People competing at the county level would progress on to the state in the specific category of competition. Categories of competition ranged from agriculture to food, handcrafts to baked goods. Ribbons were given to the top winners in their categories, with the blue ribbon signifying the highest achievement.

INGREDIENTS FOR SWEET BAKING: GRAINS

The 1860s still saw buckwheat as a favorable crop, but it was also known to help with soil fertilization and weed control. As wheat began to grow in the middle states, it started to replace buckwheat. Buckwheat had a strong flavor and a gray-like color as compared to wheat's smooth texture when fully milled, but buckwheat became, as it once had been, food for livestock. After the Civil War, the Lake Michigan area was no longer important in the growing or milling of wheat, as that had shifted west and north. Oats had a few early recorded recipes used for sweet baking.

> *OATMEAL COOKIES*
>
> *1 cup lard*
> *1 cup brown sugar*
> *1 cup molasses*
> *2 cups fine oatmeal*
> *1 teaspoon soda, dissolved in*
> *⅔ cup boiling water*
> *1 teaspoon salt*
> *1 tablespoon ginger*
> *white flour for stiff batter*
>
> *Drop in little pats in a greased dripping-pan.*
>
> *(Owens, Frances E.* Mrs. Owens' Cook Book and Useful Household Hints. *Revised and illustrated. Chicago, IL: Owens Publishing Company, 1884–85.)*

SWEETENERS

The availability of food supplies, especially sweeteners, outside of urban areas gradually improved after the Civil War. Sorghum was grown like sugar cane and harvested predominantly in the middle states up until the 1880s. When harvesting sorghum, families gathered to cut the stalks into strips. The cane stalks would be fed into a press pulled round and round by a horse. The squeezed sap ran off into wooden barrels.

"Sorghum was introduced to the United States from Africa in the early part of the seventeenth century. It was not grown extensively in this country until the 1850s, when the forage variety Black Amber (also called 'Chinese sugar cane') was introduced by way of France," according to "Sorghum—Forage."

The clearing of trees in Michigan by the lumber industry in the late 1800s brought about the beginning of the sugar beet industry. Loggers had cleared the forests, leaving behind massive tree stumps. It is now known that the sugar beets were grown from European seeds, and this could be why not all beet plants were successful in the beginning. "Official recognition by the U.S. Department of Agriculture in 1898 of the importance of the sugar beet industry sparked rapid development. One year earlier the nation had only 10 beet sugar factories…by 1900 the nationwide count stood at 30 beet sugar factories in 11 states," according to Michigan Sugar.

American housewives also carried syrup containers to the grocery store to be filled from the grocer's barrels of syrup and used this for sweet baking.

LEAVENING AGENTS

Bakers' yeast (in cake form, which required cool temperatures and was highly perishable) was introduced in 1876 at Philadelphia's Centennial Exposition. In 1882, Meadow Springs Distilling Company in Milwaukee, Wisconsin, was using yeast for the distillation of whiskey. By 1885, yeast for baking and distilling was being sold by Meadow Springs to St. Louis, Chicago and Milwaukee under a variety of names: Battle Axe, Blue Star, Lion and White Star, eventually settling on Red Star Yeast.

Salertus, Latin for aerated salt, was just that, but it was often quite bitter. The taste could be covered with grain and flour ingredients, but an acid was necessary for this agent to work. Settlers prepared their own "mix" of *saleratus*, so the end results often varied. When it was realized that sodium bicarbonate (baking soda) would release gases with the addition of an acid, experimentation began. The first use of baking powder began in about the 1830s. Baking soda plus acid (initially cream of tartar) and starch resulted in baking powder during 1843. Baking powder acted quickly with any moisture, thus the addition of starch to slow it down.

The race of baking powder and baking soda companies to promote their brands, in the late 1800s and early 1900s, resulted in a few slanderous advertisements that depicted some products as "poison like." "All baking powders that are sampled or sold with gifts may be put down as cheap lime, alum or adulterated goods, and will be avoided by prudent housekeepers," according to Abraham Morrison. Faster and simpler baking occurred with baking soda and baking powder, yielding "lighter" and new textured cakes, cookies and more.

Milk and Milk Product Methods

Until the 1850s, the dairy industry revolved around the family cow. Little dairy was sold outside the family. Louis Pasteur's pasteurization innovation in 1863 killed harmful bacteria in milk, opening up an entirely new and different dairy industry. The first dairy with pasteurization in New Jersey opened in 1891, and by 1908, Chicago had become the first city to require pasteurization for all commercial milk.

Cheese in Sweet Baking

A dairy farmer opened the first cheese factory in the United States, setting up the facility in an assembly-like fashion in 1851 in Rome, New York. This location was where neighboring farms collected and brought their milk to be fashioned into cheese.

Switzerland experienced devastation in 1844 with its dairy and, as a result, subsidized the immigration of its farmers to Wisconsin. Experienced in breeding livestock, the farmers raised dairy herds for milk and cheese. Dairy was now on its way to becoming a strong mainstay for Wisconsin folk.

In the 1860s, rennet (an enzyme that causes the milk to curdle) was mass-produced, thus allowing for more consistent cheese making. Railroads and automation also changed the small cheese/dairy farms. Products were shipped out, and the demand for cheese grew.

A cream separator was developed in Wisconsin in the 1870s. This invention resulted in butter being processed outside the home and in commercial creameries.

Cheese manufacturing had the dilemma of what to do with the whey (liquid) when making cheese. In the last century, cheese makers discovered that when whey was heated, its casein (milk protein) particles fused and created the fine white curds called ricotta.

Junket (milk with rennet)

1 quart fresh whole milk
1 junket tablet (rennet tablets)
1 tbsp. cold water
2–8 tbsp. sugar (I used 8)
1–2 tsp. vanilla extract (or to taste) or any other flavoring
dash of salt

Heat the milk in a double boiler (or in the microwave) just until lukewarm (96.8 F/37 C)—not higher than that or the milk won't set. Dissolve the sugar and salt in the milk and add the flavoring of your choice. Dissolve the rennet in cold water. Get ready 6–8 stemmed glasses. Mix the rennet water into the milk stirring very gently and very briefly and immediately pour the milk into the prepared glasses. Cover each with a piece of plastic wrap and let the milk set in a warm place. It is important not to stir, move or otherwise disturb the milk while it is setting, or the curds will separate from the whey, ruining the final result. As soon as the milk is set (it will have the consistency of a soft jelly) place the glasses in the refrigerator to chill thoroughly. Serve immediately—if the junket is left to stand it will become curdled and separate from the whey. Once ready it can be sprinkled with cinnamon or nutmeg and/or sugar.

(Stewart, Elizabeth. Lessons in Cookery: Food Economy. New York: Rand McNally and Company, 1918.)

Cream cheese, an American invention, was accidentally made by William Lawrence as he was preparing a European Neufchâtel, a soft cheese. Sold in foil wrappers from the beginning, in 1880 he named his product Philadelphia Cream Cheese. It is now a brand of the Kraft Corporation, headquartered in Illinois.

BUTTER

The first butter factories arrived in the United States in the 1860s. Competition in the wool, beef and wheat industries lowered the prices for those products. Butter making was affordable and a more profitable industry. Creameries paid farmers according to the amount of butterfat in the milk. In 1890, scientist Stephen Babcock of the University of Wisconsin invented a machine to test the butterfat quickly. This test also promoted the concept of selectively breeding specific cows for milking.

EVAPORATED AND CONDENSED MILK

Gail Borden, a New Yorker, sought a patent in 1854 to purify milk in a vacuum. Milk in the 1850s was considered a child's drink, highly perishable and likely to carry germs. Evaporating the water and condensing the milk, with the addition of sugar, yielded a safe, germ-free environment resulting in sweet and condensed milk. Borden later added evaporated milk (the same evaporation method but sugar free) to his production. This new and transportable product became a staple for Civil War soldiers.

Swiss-born John Baptist Meyenberg suggested to his company owners an evaporated milk. The idea was rejected, as the company was already successful selling condensed milk. Meyenberg took his idea to Highland, Illinois, and in 1890 he began Helvitia Milk Condensing (later PET Milk). During the Spanish-American War (1897–98), PET Milk supplied Teddy Roosevelt's Rough Riders and other American fighting troops with a safe and convenient source of milk.

SHORTENING/OILS AND FATS

In the 1870s, various patents of formulas for shortenings were introduced, including the first shortening made with vegetable oils and fats. A process to deodorize cottonseed oil for cooking and baking was marketed as Snowdrift by the Southern Oil Company but was later named for its chemist, David Wesson. In the 1920s, Wesson Oil & Snowdrift Company began a vegetable oil division. Legislation rose to control food adulteration. The 1880s experienced the first food testing for safety. Snowdrift was the first commercial all-vegetable shortening used. Primarily used by commercial bakeries rather than households at this time, the oil shortenings were sold in bulk to trade.

Margarine was accidentally "discovered" but also researched on purpose by French scientists in response to a demand by Emperor Louis Napoleon III in 1869 for alternative fats and oils, as there was a shortage. Suet plus milk solids resulted in the first palatable margarine. Mark Twain contributed a conversation in his book *Life on the Mississippi*, which had two businessmen discussing margarine: "Why, we are turning out oleomargarine now, by the thousands of tons. And we can sell it so dirt-cheap that the whole country has got to take it—can't get around it, you see. Butter don't stand any show—there ain't any chance for competition."

Margarine experienced extensive anti-legislation, but a federal Margarine Act in 1886 secured product "wholesomeness" (no adulteration). The focus was on butter substitutes and butter rather than lard and lard substitutes. This movement proved to promote margarine further ahead than the use of lard in baking and cooking. Margarine rapidly caught on in the United States and Europe, where many people began to seek patents. Large-scale production was underway by the 1870s. The margarine industry purchased much of the good-quality lard, leaving the lard refiners with lard that was too soft. In order to harden the lard, low-quality oils were added, and the consumers began to turn away. Chicago had a strong presence in animal "fat" production. During this time, a majority of the nation's meatpacking industry was located there. Armour and Company, in the 1880s, became the first large meatpacker to refine its own lard and shortening and eventually moved into cottonseed oil mills and refineries.

EARLY THICKENING METHODS

Arrowroot was a plant that European settlers and explorers discovered in the New World. The tuberous rhizome was highly starchy and nutritious. It also had medicinal values. The tuber, aru-aru, evolved into our present-day "arrowroot," as wounds inflicted by poisonous arrows healed with the application of the tuber.

> ### MRS. HALE'S ARROWROOT PUDDING
> ### (CIVIL WAR ERA)
>
> *In 1 cup of milk mix 3 tablespoons of arrowroot. Then stir it into 3 cups of boiling milk. Allow to cool; then stir in four beaten eggs, 2 ounces of granulated sugar, and 2 ounces of butter. Stir until the butter is melted. Then add 1 teaspoon of nutmeg. Pour into a greased baking dish or pan, and bake 20 minutes at 400 F, or until knife inserted in the center comes out clean.*
>
> (Davis, Willliam. A Taste for War. Mechanicsburg, PA: Stackpole Books, 2003.)

Gelatin preparation—boiling and reducing liquids from the bones and intestines of animals—was a long and arduous process. The Victorian era fashioned gelatin molds into works of edible art. From the 1840s onward, various people attempted patents on a gelatin, eventually morphing gelatin into fruit flavors, a far cry from the original boiled carcasses. Gelatin was sold as granules quite close to the current form found in contemporary grocery shops.

FRUIT

The early settlers lived at considerable distances from one another, and gatherings were infrequent. Social gatherings based around harvests were eagerly awaited in the social life of the Great Plains. Spring's strawberry yield might garner a group for strawberry shortcake. "Strawberries were only briefly and seasonally abundant until the development of north-south railroads extended the season for urban cooks. This made for strawberry shortcake parties in the 1840s, but printed recipes did not reach cookbooks right away," according to the History Cook website.

As the sugar beet growers took advantage of the cleared land, so did the fruit

Blueberry, peach and apple growers began to take advantage of the cleared land, and a booming fruit industry began in South Haven, Michigan, in the 1870s–1900s. *Historyofsouthhaven.org.*

growers. A Presbyterian minister planted the first commercial tart cherry orchards in 1893 on a farm in Michigan, known to some as the "Fruit Belt."

Saugatuck and Douglas, Michigan, located on Lake Michigan's eastern shores, joined in with the planting of orchards in the late 1800s. Originally, lumber was shipped across the lake to rebuild Chicago after the Great Fire in 1871. South Haven, Michigan, also began to cultivate blueberries, apples and peaches, filling the barren land. New industries for canning and cider mills resulted from fruit harvests. Now orchards yielded fruit, especially peaches called "Michigan Gold"; these, too, were steam shipped across to Chicago and Milwaukee.

A peach disease, called the Yellows, devastated this area's trees and fruits in the 1870s. It took until the turn of the century for the fruit growers to rebuild their orchards. By the early 1900s, the tart cherry industry was established in the state and processed fruit shipped to Chicago, Detroit and Milwaukee.

NUTS

In the United States, the pecans are second in popularity only to peanuts (not really a nut); this country produces about 80 percent of the world's pecans. Pecans come in a variety of sizes, and there are in excess of one thousand varieties of pecans.

The peanut, native to South America, found its way to America by way of North Carolina. Dr. John Kellogg from the Battle Creek Sanitarium in Michigan prepared the peanut nutmeats for his patients and patented the process in 1895. Peanut butter was prepared and served at the health sanitarium. *The Complete Guide to Nut Cookery*, published in 1899, further propagated the great uses for peanuts, and many companies made peanut butter in 1914.

FLAVORINGS

The cocoa plant and chocolate were never indigenous to the middle states, but they did have a special presence in Chicago during the World's Columbian Exposition in 1893. East Coast cocoa and chocolate producers brought (New England's) Baker's chocolate for sampling and drinking. What was most world-changing was the chocolate enrobing machine. The Swiss quickly took this concept back to Europe and worked on perfecting enrobing chocolates (a process by which a machine poured chocolate over a soft chocolate candy, and the fluid chocolate covered and coated it, keeping it fresh and easily transported). Ultimately, this machine catapulted the chocolate making business into the public eye. Now, consuming a chocolate treat was more than a special occasion. Chocolate became more readily available in sweet baked items, but more so for candy makers.

PERIOD-SPECIFIC SWEET BAKED GOODS: CIVIL WAR TASTES

Civil War recipes certainly did not move the sweet baked repertoire forward; rather, the war revealed tastes and traditions from the South and North to one another. These recipes were gathered from newspapers and publications of the era: "Confederate Molasses Pie, Josephine Peffer's 1860 Wisconsin Gingerbread, Confederate Apple Pie Without the Apples, and Mrs. Rutledge's Sweet Potato Pone," according to William Davis's *A Taste for War*.

During the Civil War, we also saw the first community cookbook, *A Poetical Cookbook*, by Maria J. Moss, dedicated to the Sanitary Fair held for the soldiers and their families and published in 1864. Community cookbooks display a more detailed and regional look at culinary traditions. Churches, schools and charities often began first with a bake sale or community dinner or an event where favored foods became the printed recipe version. These recipes reveal the true foods prepared, shared and enjoyed by many Americans, as opposed to a cookbook commercially produced.

During this time, many cookie varieties had similar names: Gingerbread, Molasses, Ginger Snaps, Spice and Sand Tarts (a butter cookie with delicately placed almonds on top). The Hermit cookie was also written down. The cookie's origin has ties, by some, to twelfth-century Europe, but for American purposes, it was included in Fannie Farmer's 1896 cookbook and was still printed by community cookbooks in Michigan all the way into the 1930s. Hermits might have derived from extra baking ingredients—it's a firm cookie, travels easily and is always delightful when hungry.

Fannie Farmer's cookbook never indicated how thick to roll these cookies. It is also interesting to note that raisins had seeds at this time. A specially designed tool was used to de-seed the raisins. Later, Hermit cookie recipes added nuts.

> *HERMITS*
>
> ½ cup butter
> ½ cup raisins, stoned and cut into
>   small pieces
> ⅔ cup sugar
> ½ teaspoon cinnamon
> 1 egg
> ¼ teaspoon clove
> 2 tablespoons milk
> ¼ teaspoon mace
> 2 teaspoons baking powder
> ¼ teaspoon nutmeg
>
> *Cream the butter and add sugar gradually, then the raisins, the egg well beaten and the milk. Mix and sift dry ingredients and add to first mixture. Roll mixture a little thicker than for Vanilla wafers. 350 F. for 8–10 minutes until lightly browned.*

Middle State Flavors

Sweet baking began to take on a middle state and American "flavor." Ingredients like oats that may have been used only by specific immigrant groups were now marketed to new groups of Americans by new companies. Quaker Oats promoted its breakfast ingredient as one for sweet baking. At one point, company wars over oatmeal yielded a bigger and stronger Quaker Oats, which printed the first recipe on the outside of a box.

Originally, children were thought of as "little adults" and did not have toys, much less special children's parties. The late 1800s exhibited a change in home and social attitudes toward children. Parties, toys and celebrations began to include the celebratory cake. Cakes brought to America were European-style "enriched yeast doughs," buttery with special fruits. Now the middle states celebrated birthdays by preparing contemporary cakes with frosting and perhaps even ice cream.

Fruit tarts in Europe became fruit pies in the middle states. Fillings in pies reflected indigenous ingredients. In plentiful times, fruits, berries and custards might fill a pie crust. When food was scarce or harvests eaten, pies reflected "simple" fillings, with what might be left in the cupboard. Early pies were not vastly different from the ones we eat today. Seasonal fruits and sometimes vegetables, especially pumpkin and squash (new to the settlers), as well as basic custards with eggs, creams and soft cheeses, were fillings for pies. Pies that used a sweetener varied as more ingredients were available. The availability of food supplies, especially sweeteners, outside of urban areas gradually improved after the Civil War. The Midwest earned a reputation as the "pie belt." "By the twentieth century, 'pie tins' were cheap and common. Some incorporated a rotating pin to release the bottom crust," according to Alice Ross at the Journal of Antiques website.

The Sugar Cream Pie recipe appears to have originated in Indiana with the Shaker and/or Amish communities in the 1800s. This was a great pie recipe to use when the apple bins were empty. Danish kringles (a pastry dough filled with fruits and/or nuts, covered with icing), having a distinct oval shape, were prepared in the late 1800s. Racine, Wisconsin, was home to a large Danish population with an interesting sweet history. In Denmark, a bakery sign is indicated with a pretzel-shaped kringle. Over time, the pastry dough shape morphed into an oval here in the United States, so now the dough is overlapped and entirely filled with sweet fillings and sometimes nuts.

"The kringles were created by German bakers from Austria who introduced their method of rolling butter between layers of yeast dough and letting it rest for hours before baking. When Danish bakers in Copenhagen went on strike, the bakery owners fired them and hired replacements from Austria. Once the Danish bakers returned to their jobs, they continued to make dough the Austrian way," according to the What's Cooking America website.

Coffeecakes, and sweet cakes are prepared with a simple dough or an enriched sweet dough (butter and yeast). What else could accompany this but a lovely coffee or sweet wine. Scandinavians, Austrians, Germans and the Dutch and French brought their sweet recipes with them to the Lake Michigan states. At first, these doughs were far denser, as in kugelhopf, kuchen or gugelhupf—flour, yeast, sugar, dried fruit, spices and sometimes nuts. Recipes changed over time, using ingredients from their new home such as soft cheese fillings, jams and preserves. Topped with pecans and black walnuts, this became an American-style coffeecake. Midwestern states with German populations had many commercial bakeries, including such sweet baked goods as coffeecakes and crumb-topped streusel kuchen and apfelkuchen or other fruit-decorated yeast cakes. For toppings, they used cherries, peaches or plums, as well as apples.

SWEET CELEBRATIONS

Celebrations and fairs, such as the World's Columbian Exposition, in Chicago in 1893, also contributed to the American sweet palate. About 20.7 million people attended the fair from May through October 1893. Inhabitants from the Midwest, Northeast, South and the newer West United States traveled to Chicago to experience many fascinating and life-changing inventions: electricity, indoor plumbing, chewing gum, caramel corn, hot dogs, a Ferris wheel and many more. Souvenir cookbooks were also printed, exemplifying recipes of the era.

COLUMBIAN EXPOSITION RECIPES

Carrie Shuman's *Favorite Dishes: A Columbian Autograph Souvenir*, from the World's Columbian Exposition in Chicago, Illinois, in 1893, gathered recipes from the "Lady Managers" from around the United States. Miss Frances E. Willard of Illinois included an explanation beforehand for her mother's doughnuts.

FAMOUS DOUGHNUTS

To tell you the truth, I never knew anything about cooking or had a particle of taste for it, but I will send you the recipe for her famous "doughnuts," written out by my beloved mother, and I think about the last communication she ever prepared for the press; it was in March of last year. There is nothing specially valuable about the recipe except that it is good and decidedly old fashioned. I used to think there was nothing so toothsome as mother's "fried cakes," for so we called them on the old Wisconsin farm. Believe me, yours, with all good wishes,

Frances Willard

Take a little over one pint of rich, sweet milk, into which put two-thirds of a teacup of sugar and a little salt. Sift as much flour as you think will be required, into which mix four heaping teaspoonfuls of best baking powder. Stir into the milk and sugar six tablespoonfuls of very hot fresh lard, pour the mixture into the flour and make a sponge. When cooled sufficiently to prevent cooking the egg add one egg slightly beaten. Mix to a proper consistency, roll and cut into rings. It is hard to give a recipe where so much depends upon the judgement and care of the cook. Much depends upon having the lard in which the doughnuts are fried very hot before they are put in, otherwise they "soak up the fat" and are heavy.

CHOCOLATE FUDGE BROWNIES

America can thank the Palmer House for inventing its favorite dessert.

1 pound and ¼ cup semi-sweet chocolate
1 pound butter
1½ cups granulated sugar
1 cup cake flour
1 tablespoon baking powder
4 whole eggs
1 pound crushed walnuts

Melt chocolate with butter in a double boiler. Mix all dry ingredients except walnuts into mixing bowl. Mix chocolate with dry ingredients, 4 to 5 minutes. Add eggs. Pour into 9 x 12-inch baking sheet, sprinkle walnuts on top, press walnuts down slightly into mixture with your hand and bake in a preheated oven at 300 degrees for 30 to 40 minutes. You will know when it is done when the edges start to become a little crispy and the brownies have risen to about ¼ inch. Remove from the oven and allow to cool for about 30 minutes before spreading it with a thick layer of glaze with a pastry brush.

GLAZE
1 cup water
1 cup apricot preserves
1 teaspoon unflavored gelatin

Mix water, preserves and unflavored gelatin in a saucepan. Mix thoroughly and bring to a boil for two minutes. Use hot.

Special tip: The brownies are easier to cut if you place in the freezer for about 3 to 4 hours after glazing.

Note: The first reference to the "brownie" in America appears in the *Sears Roebuck Catalog* published in Chicago 1898. Specifically at the direction of Bertha Palmer to be served at the Columbian Exposition World Fair in 1893, the brownie was created in the Palmer House Kitchen in the late nineteenth century. This recipe is well over a century old and is the exact same one used for the brownie served at the Palmer House Hilton today. It remains one of the hotel's most popular confections.

THE LESAFFRE GROUP

I suppose writing inquiry e-mails and researching material are what many teachers do to prepare for class. On my quests for information for my baking classes, I have contacted various companies and personnel over the years, but one particular quest for information proved very different. As I navigated the Red Star–Lesaffre website, I noticed that they had already "personalized" the e-mail questions. It seemed as though someone named Carol Stevens was the one person responsible for responding to the questions. Thank goodness…one person might be answering my request, I thought. A most prompt reply from "Carol" began a conversation that lasted many months. Our similar interest in baking perhaps? Our ties to the Midwest and Milwaukee? Regardless, I enjoyed our conversations about sweet baking, yeast, delicious recipes and our lives in the food and baking industry. This was a delightful meeting of shared common interests. Many of you bakers and baking aficionados may recognize Red Star Yeast, as it is an icon in the baking aisle.

Founded in 1882 as Meadow Springs Distilling Company in Milwaukee, Wisconsin, the merger of distilling and yeast making was a natural match. Not only was yeast needed for distillation, grains could

CRANBERRY NUT BREAD

Cranberries and spices add a festive touch; oatmeal adds moistness. Especially good toasted.

5½ cups to 6 cups all-purpose flour
2 (¼ ounce) packets RED STAR® active dry yeast
1 cup oatmeal, dry
½ cup sugar
1½ teaspoons salt
1 teaspoon ground allspice
1 teaspoon mace
1½ cups milk
¼ cup butter or vegetable oil
1 large egg
2 cups coarsely chopped cranberries
½ cup raisins
½ cup chopped nuts

Preheat oven to 350 degrees. In large mixer bowl, combine 2½ cups flour, yeast, oatmeal, sugar, salt, allspice and mace; mix well. Combine milk, water and butter or oil; heat until very warm (120 to 130 degrees; butter does not need to melt). Add to flour mixture. Add egg. Blend at low speed until moistened; beat 3 minutes at medium speed. Using your hands, gradually stir in cranberries, raisins, nuts and enough remaining flour to make a firm dough. Knead on floured surface for 5 to 8 minutes. Place in greased bowl, turning to grease top. Cover; let rise in warm place until almost double and holes remain from fingers inserted into dough, about 1 hour.

Punch down dough; divide into 2 parts. On lightly floured surface, roll or pat each half to a 14 x 7-inch rectangle. Starting with the shorter side, roll up tightly, pressing dough into roll with each turn. Pinch edges and ends to seal. Place in greased 9 x 5-inch bread pans. Cover; let rise in warm place until indentation remains after lightly touching side of loaf, about 1 hour. Bake at 350 degrees for 40 to 45 minutes, until deep golden brown. Remove from pans; cool. Makes 2 loaves.

Tip: Cranberries can be easily chopped in a blender or food processor.

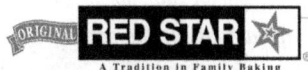

ORIGINAL **RED STAR** ★
A Tradition in Family Baking

Kelly Olson, Red Star–Lesaffre Yeast Corporation,
Milwaukee, Wisconsin

Q. Your name and job title at Red Star–Lesaffre Corporation?
A. Kelly Olson, Consumer Relations. My "persona" is Carol Stevens—I answer customer's questions through e-mail and on the telephone. I have worked for Red Star–Lesaffre for almost twenty years in Milwaukee, Wisconsin, at their North America headquarters.

Q. How did you become involved with Red Star–Lesaffre Corporation?
A. I am a Midwesterner who majored in chemistry. I worked with a Baker's Co-op for a number of years in Chicago and decided I would like to focus on one ingredient—yeast. I joined Red Star in 1992.

Q. What is the story behind your persona, "Carol Stevens"?
A. Carol Stevens, initials stand for Customer Service. Her persona/illustration can be found on the Red Star–Lesaffre website. Her character evolved in the 1950s. A warm smile and grandmother-like "look," she has transformed into the Betty Crocker of yeast. Carol (Kelly now) answers consumer's questions about Red Star–Lesaffre products, as well as baking questions.

Q. What have been some of your most memorable questions?
A. One day, a grandmother called to ask if it was harmful to drink yeast. As it turned out, she was making her grandson's favorite cinnamon rolls and had mixed her yeast with warm water and sugar and left the cup sitting on the counter to proof. When she returned to the kitchen, she found the cup empty. Turns out, her grandson had found the cup, thought it was chocolate milk and drank the whole thing! Needless to say, her fourteen-year-old grandson missed out on the cinnamon rolls and instead passed a lot of gas for a couple of days!

Q. Have consumers' questions changed over the years? Or have they been about the same?
A. Let's face it, some people are very intimidated by yeast, and there's a lot of confusion out there about yeast and how to use it. To me it's important to not only answer the question but to take the time to explain and educate about yeast and its role in dough making so that the person can learn to bake with confidence. Overall, the questions remain about the same from year to year, but in recent years, I get more and more questions from men. Interestingly, though, they tend to approach it like an engineering

project and want more detailed information about the process, the ingredients, dough consistency, etc.

Q. Have you observed changes in consumers' behaviors over the years? Or in other words, have sales and products purchased changed during World War I and II, the Depression or any recessions in the United States?
A. Baking at home has changed over the years. During recessions and depressions, it increases. During the 1960s, as women entered the workforce, less baking at home occurred. In the 1980s, bread machines exhibited an increase in home baking again. The last several years have shown an increase in baking for varying reasons: health, natural ingredients and a slower economy.

Q. What inventions and products did Red Star–Lesaffre create due to industrialization?
A. In the 1920s, Red Star manufactured aerated yeast, which was promoted for nutritional health. During World War II, the United States government sponsorship encouraged the company's scientific exploration to develop a yeast that needed low moisture and no refrigeration. Dry active yeast was the result, which enabled the military overseas to use this product in its mobile kitchens. Further advancements have been made in recent years in the use of yeast in human nutrition, pharmaceuticals and animal nutrition.

Q. Do you want to share any specific "recipe" that reflects Midwest sweet flavors or traditions?
A. Cranberry Nut Bread is from the Historical Red Star Recipe File. Surprisingly, it sounds contemporary and is still quite popular. Cranberries are a fruit from Wisconsin, and depending on the nut, that, too, can be from the Midwest.

also be sold for animal feed. By 1885, 200,000 pounds of yeast was being sold to St. Louis, Chicago and, of course, Milwaukee. Blue Star, White Star and Battle Axe were a few early names of this yeast company. Prohibition shuttered distilling but fueled the demand for marketing yeast to bakers. The world wars and industrialization yielded new inventions and new owner, as the Lesaffre Group acquired Red Star in 2001, continuing the tradition of leadership in the science of yeast. A recent trend has been the demand for gluten-free products. Red Star–Lesaffre has responded by meeting these demands with products and recipes.

Kelly shared two recipes from the Historical Red Star Recipe File. Cranberry Nut Bread is displayed here, while the Apple Kuchen is in the contemporary recipes chapter.

Chapter 4

War and Industrialization, 1900-1939

Crossing Cultures

Industrialization opened the twentieth century with inventions that affected food directly. Food production was faster, less expensive and easier. Factories now began to produce breads, crackers and sweet bakery products. Larger companies absorbed some small bakeries. By 1906, the eight-year-old National Biscuit Company (renamed Nabisco) was earning about $40 million annually. About 1,300 men and women were employed at the Chicago bakeries.

Independent and commercial bakeries had a number of professional organizations to participate in for myriad reasons at the turn of the century. Bakery and confectionery workers united, designating Chicago as headquarters in 1904. Union membership steadily increased, with an all-time high in the 1940s nearing eighty thousand nationwide. The Retail Bakers of America, another professional organization, founded in 1918, partnered sellers and buyers for profitable bakeries, as well as offered training for the industry, apprenticeships and mentorships among bakers. The organization also helped formulate industry standards and industry research.

The government's involvement with food was both at the demand of consumers as well as a shock reaction when local and national food inspections saw chaos. The 1906 Food and Drug Act "prohibited interstate commerce in misbranded and adulterated foods, drinks, and drugs." Upton Sinclair's book about Chicago's meatpacking industry, *The Jungle*, prompted the Meat Inspection Act. This worked to prevent adulterated or misbranded meat and meat products from being sold as food and to ensure that meat and meat products were slaughtered and processed under sanitary conditions.

Although the law focused on meat products, food companies were now being held to a production standard. Child labor laws also gave guidelines for a working age, fourteen years old, as well as a specified wage.

Cities were growing in size, but there was still a strong agricultural community, and the U.S. government recognized this. The Smith-Lever Act in 1914 created a Cooperative Extension System at the United States Department of Agriculture (USDA). This system ensured that cooperatives would teach agriculture, home economics and related subjects. These groups organized and became the 4-H Clubs.

Canned foods and imported foods, with the addition of cookbooks, mixed foods' seasonality and blended cultures through recipes. Canned peaches in January now could yield peach pie in winter. Food manufacturers, including those who produced products for sweet baked goods, challenged consumers through recipe contests, welcoming the "melting pot" of culinary repertoires from farm folk to city dwellers. New food traditions plus old food traditions resulted in new recipes.

Women who had traditionally spent most of their day farming and cooking could now purchase foods and baked items that may have been made at home before. Their time was freer to entertain and socialize—this meant cooking and baking or purchasing products already made to serve to guests.

WORLD WAR I

World War I was unexpected and challenging. America's involvement was shocking at first. The Lake Michigan states were not immune from the shortages and rationing of products, including food.

Noted the Historical Boys' Clothing website

> *When the United States entered the War, President Wilson appointed Herbert Hoover to the post of United States Food Administrator (1917). Food had become a weapon in World War I and no country produced more food than America. Hoover succeeded in cutting consumption of foods needed overseas and avoided rationing at home, yet kept the Allies fed. America had to produce the food needed by the new large army America was building as well as for Allied armies and civilians.*

Food conservation occurred through messages sent by the "new" U.S. Food Administration. Wheatless and meatless days were encouraged. War gardens, better known as victory gardens, promoted the public working together to produce food to relieve pressure on the supply, but it also gave a common support for the war effort at home. Wheat was such an important world commodity that the U.S. government began to control the use of it, as well as the use of sugar. The government did not use the word "ration," although these two commodities were heavily guarded.

THE GREAT DEPRESSION

The stock market crash in 1929 began a devastating, four-year spiral downward. Unemployment in cities and in agriculture touched almost every American, as well as people worldwide. The Great Plains, including parts of Wisconsin, Indianan, Illinois and Michigan, were also suffering from drought conditions. Fifty million acres had been wasted by 1933 from the combination of the Depression and drought. The Dust Bowl created drastic conditions; heat and winds contributed to the abandoned lands. Land that was unused now suffered from erosion, more than 100 millions acres' worth. What was happening to this once fertile land?

Congress created the Soil Conservation Service in 1935. New projects were developed to stop soil erosion and renew the fertility; crop rotation and new plants were some of the measures needed to "bring back" these once abundant lands.

MIGRATION QUOTAS

"In the first census of the 20th century, the population of the United States rose to 76,212,168, a 21 percent increase since 1890. For the first time, all fifty entities that would become the fifty states are included after Hawaii had officially become a territory of the United States on February 22," according to the America's Best History website.

The Great Migration of African Americans in the 1920s occurred when the majority moved into urban areas from the southern United States to Chicago, Detroit, St. Louis and Milwaukee. Southern foodways brought many savory traditions, as well as sweet "soul food" contributions—most renowned are the sweet potato pie and pecan pie. Sweet potato pie is believed to have originated from the African slave trade being mixed with European foodways. When these traditions were combined, new recipes evolved.

The 1924 Immigration Act was a law limiting the annual number of immigrants admitted from any country to 2 percent of the number of people from that country who were already living in the United States. Quotas reduced Italian immigration, but Germany, Britain and Ireland had the most reductions. The biggest immigration wave from Italy in 1910 brought a majority of the Italians to Milwaukee and Chicago. This is not to say that Italians did not live elsewhere; rather, many of their skills with food preparation, including pastry and confections, gave them a rapid way to find employment in those cities. Many Italians opened restaurants, grocery stores, pastry shops and bakeries. Although 5.3 million immigrated over the span of forty years, one-third returned to Italy after five years. "For many [Germans] the major change was the shift from skilled to semiskilled work, as the skilled baker preparing bread and making cakes in the 1880s had given way to the machine tender in a bread or cracker factory 20 years later," according to Christiane Harzig.

INVENTIONS

Electricity available in urban areas first gave consumers new ways to store food. Gas stoves replaced wood and fuel stoves and ovens. The first effective thermostat could regulate baking heat in 1915 for a gas stove. By the 1920s, electric stove manufacturers had also implemented a thermostat. Sweet baking at home now had a more reliable heat source. The first airplane appeared in 1914, as well as mainstream automobiles. Refrigerators and stoves were common in most homes by the 1930s. "The value of geographically separate bakeries operating under a single organization had proven its worth with the advent of the automobile. A fleet of trucks enabled the locally oriented bakeries to develop into regional bakeries, providing the locomotion for a territory-widening distribution system," according to the Funding Universe website.

The hand-held eggbeater, invented in the mid-nineteenth century, was one step toward the invention of the mixer, which came in 1908 as the first electric mixer, eventually growing into two types of models, counter or stand. Commercial bakeries could produce large-volume batches using attachments for different methods; paddle, whisk and dough hooks also reduced the dependency on skilled labor.

During this time, the state of Michigan yielded two influential names in sweet baking. Perhaps not recognized as sweet bakers immediately, both companies affected the use of traditional breakfast cereals in sweet baking recipes.

In 1895, Postum Cereal Company gained notoriety for its powdered, roasted grain beverage, a substitute for coffee, which became very popular during the rationing of coffee in World War II. Cooking and baking competitions, using cereal items, marketed these products. Monetary prizes and notoriety through recipe winners in booklets garnered attention and fame for everyday Americans. Cereals were no longer just for breakfast. Consumers could use these products throughout the day, including in their sweet baked products.

Postum Cereal Plant, Battle Creek, Michigan. *Author's private collection.*

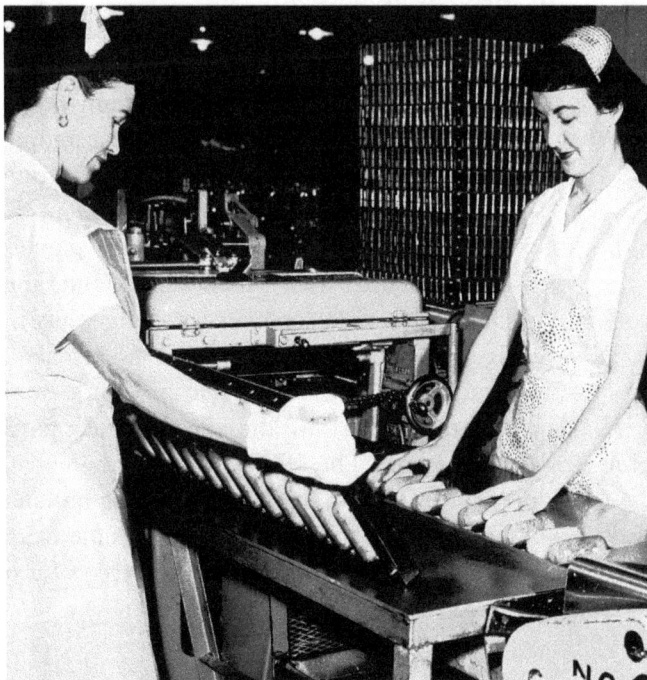

"In the early days, every Twinkie had to be hand filled using a specially created machine operated with a food pedal. You had to pump the pedal just right, or too much filling would shoot out." *Hostess Brands.*

GRAPE-NUTS RAISIN CAKE

1 ¾ cups sifted Swans Down Cake Flour
1 teaspoon baking powder
1 teaspoon soda
1 teaspoon salt
½ teaspoon nutmeg
1 cup warm water
1 cup Grape-Nuts
1 teaspoon cinnamon
½ cup butter or other shortening
1 cup brown sugar
2 eggs, well beaten
1 cup raisins, floured

Sift flour once, measure, add baking powder, soda, salt, cinnamon, and nutmeg and sift three times. Pour warm water over Grape-Nuts. Cream shortening thoroughly, add sugar gradually, and cream together until light and fluffy. Add eggs, then sift dry ingredients alternately with water and Grape-Nuts, a small amount at a time. Beat well after each addition. Add raisins. Bake in greased loaf pan (5 x 10 x 3 inches) in moderate oven (350 F) 1 hour.

(This recipe received $500 for third prize. It was submitted for a competition sponsored by Postum Company. 101 Prize Recipes. N.p.: Postum Company Incorporated, 1928.)

The Grape-Nuts cereal proved successful, but "Elijah Manna Flakes Cereal" did not find immediate fame quite as expected; by renaming them Post Toasties, consumers were sold.

Another newly founded company in 1906, Kellogg, ironically by the sanitarium where C.W. Post resided for health restoration, became known for its Battle Creek Toasted Corn Flakes. Eventually, it was marketed and produced as Kellogg's Toasted Corn Flakes.

How about "roadside marketing"? Nature's bounty was sold on the side of the road in the form of fruits, jellies, milk, butter, buttermilk and maple syrup. As cars became accessible, people drove to rural areas and purchased what the government protected through a 1914 Michigan Roadside Market Association, enforcing food standards for roadside production.

Novelty cookies, created by Nabisco, were modeled after P.T Barnum's circus. In 1902, the cookies were marketed as ornaments to hang from the Christmas tree. The animal crackers came in a boxed cage with a string attached, which doubled as the ornament.

During the Depression, many parcels of farmland were abandoned. But the Depression did propagate some ingenuity in the creation of newly formed sweet baked goods. Mr. James Dewar, from Continental Bakery in Illinois, suggested a bakery item that would use the idle shortcake pans that had only been used during strawberry season. The 1930s proved a challenge, and people were frugal in a slow economy. Mr. Dewar suggested injecting banana filling in the oblong golden cakes. The name "Twinkie" is said to have come from a billboard that Mr. Dewar saw advertising "Twinkle Toe Shoes." Two cakes for a nickel and the jazzier Twinkie name equaled success.

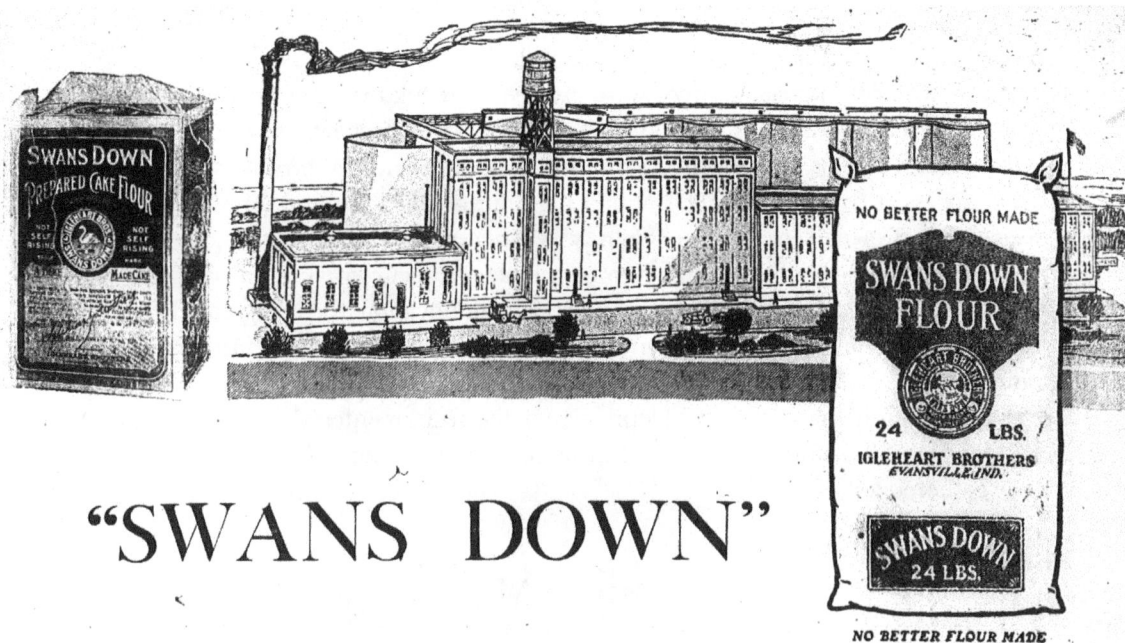

"SWANS DOWN"

Igleheart advertisement, Evansville, Indiana, 1917. *HistoricEvansville.com.*

Sweet Baking Ingredients

The era between 1900 and 1939 experienced such extremes. Industrialized ingredients and the mass production of food made it accessible to all regions in the middle states. Yet the world wars and Depression minimalized accessibility of certain ingredients, too, like flour, sugar and butter—the staples and very essence of sweet baked goods. Not all war efforts were negative, though, which we can see in vitamin- and mineral-enriched flour and canned milk. The Midwest prevailed in moving forward using the fruits of the land and hard work and ingenuity from desperate situations.

Fruit and Nut Traditions

In the 1900s, nuts made the transition from a dessert food to an important component of the American diet. This trend was advanced by the U.S. Department of Agriculture, which published numerous recipes and booklets with diverse recipes that used nuts as the main ingredients. Kitchen notes from an old-time farm magazine (circa 1915) talk of nut sandwiches using walnuts, pecans and hickory nuts for the school lunchbox. Recipes from commercial sources were also being regularly published in magazines and mainstream cookbooks, such as *Eight Hundred Proved Pecan Recipes.*

By the early 1900s, the tart cherry industry was established in the state of Michigan, and processed fruit was being shipped to Chicago, Detroit and Milwaukee. The fruit orchard owners of Berrien County, Michigan, had previously encountered a devastating yellow blight, yet now another challenge occurred: a bitter frost in 1906. Most helpful (and challenging) was an unexpected innovation: the refrigerated railroad car. Now fruit could be brought to customers in the middle states from further growing points outside of the Michigan area. Competition had arrived!

Stories are told that during the Depression native fruits reentered the local foodways. Pawpaws and persimmons, not used in popular sweet baking during this era, were now gathered for sustenance.

Canned Milk

Remember PET Milk in Illinois? In 1934, it was the first company to irradiate canned milk, and Vitamin D was fortified in the process. Pasteurization relies on heat, and irradiation relies on the energy of ionizing radiation.

Sweeteners: Sugar

After World War I, refined sugar prices dropped, and consumers and the industry switched to white and brown sugar. Recipes in the 1900s sometimes suggest that brown sugar was infested with bugs. Never again did people consume the quantities of molasses that were once available. Sugar consumption was on the rise, but now sugar cane production had competition with the rise of sugar beet production.

Sugar beet factories began to open around the nation, and by 1910 they out produced sugar cane. The early attempts at growing beets in Europe taught ideas about crop rotation, fertilizing and also ways to supply food for livestock. About 1,500

From the Hotel St. Francis Cook Book by Victor Hirtzler, 1919, Chicago, Illinois.

Menu for June 6
Souffle glace, Pavlowa. Whip a pint of rich cream until thick. Beat the yolks of four eggs with one-quarter pound of sugar, until very light. Then add it to the cream, with a pony of maraschino. Whip the whites of five eggs very hard, and add them to the mixture, mixing lightly. Then fill fancy paper cases until about one inch higher than the edges, and set to freeze. When hard, and just before serving, dip the tops in grated lemon.

pounds of seeds were brought to Michigan from France. Tree stumps were cleared from the now bygone era of lumbering, and the success of sugar beets began. In the early years, sugar beets proved to be one of the more profitable crops per acre. The merging of various beet sugar companies and farmers over the years developed into the Michigan Sugar Company, a one-thousand-farmer co-op producing under two labels, Pioneer Sugar and Big Chief Sugar.

CORN SYRUP

In 1902, a chemist and expert syrup formulator named his syrup "Karo" after his wife, Caroline. The Corn Products Refining Company of New York and Chicago was formed, introducing Karo Light and Dark Corn Syrup.

BAKING THICKENERS

What one sees through "modern" food products is a past of trials and errors, some edible and some not. This certainly stands true for gelatin. As mentioned, the boiling of animal carcasses progressed until cough syrup manufacturer Pearl Wait's wife renamed the newer inventions of dessert "Jell-O." Success? No, not immediately, but by 1906, sales had caught on. Recipe books and celebrities connected to special recipes moved this "special occasion" gelatin into more common usage. Jell-O also was put into various sweet baked products.

FLAVORINGS: SALT

> *PECAN PIE*
>
> ½ cup butter
> ½ cup sugar
> 3 eggs
> 1 cup pecan nutmeats
> ½ cup white corn syrup
> 1 teaspoon vanilla
> ½ cup maple syrup
> unbaked pie shell
>
> *Work butter until creamy; add sugar, syrups, and eggs well beaten. Mix well, add nutmeats, broken in pieces, and vanilla. Pour into 8-inch pie shell and bake one hour in a moderate oven 325 to 350 F., or until knifepoint comes out clean. Serve with whip cream if desired.*
>
> (Mrs. N.J. Brodeur, from Houghton, Michigan, circa 1930.)

Health in the region around the Great Lakes and Pacific Northwest exhibited a prevalence of goiters. A professor of pediatrics at the University of Michigan championed the cause to improve this phenomenon with the addition of potassium iodide or sodium iodide to cooking and table salt. Michigan led the nation with the first iodized salt in May 1924. Morton Salt Company, in Chicago, Illinois, began distributing the iodized salt nationally by the fall of 1924.

Period-Specific Sweet Baked Goods

At first, the 1900s yielded an abundance of butter, sugar, spices and flour, reasonably priced. A variety of leavening agents, such as baking powder and baking soda, also yielded consistent and flavorful sweet baked products. "Koekje," the Dutch word for "little cake," was what we began to call our present-day cookies. Cookbooks and shared recipes up until this time had many similar-style cookies. Now, ovens with regulated temperatures plus reliable and fresh ingredients resulted in new varieties of cookies.

"Cocoanut" was the early word for what is called coconut today. No one is certain as to when it exactly changed to the present spelling, but it is noticeable that the spelling was very close to the word "cocoa." As more cocoa was introduced into recipes, a differentiation may have been made.

"Fair food" may conjure images of corn dogs and cotton candy. But the state of Wisconsin created something that now delights fair attendees in the land of dairy. In 1924, the Wisconsin Baker's Association and the State of Wisconsin began a venture to operate a live bakery during the state fair. The Dairy Bakery produced foods to showcase Wisconsin's dairy industry. The glass window allowed people to observe the bakers' skills and quantity of production—and of course, people could also taste the end results.

> ### Cocoanut Bars
>
> ½ cup butter
> 1 cup flour
> ¼ teaspoon salt
>
> Mix as a pie crust. Press into a pan and bake for 10 minutes at 350 F.
>
> #### Filling
> 2 eggs beaten until light
> 1 teaspoon baking powder
> 1½ cups light brown sugar
> 1 cup cocoanut
> 1 teaspoon vanilla
> ½ cup nutmeats
> 7 teaspoons flour
>
> Prepare filling and drop from a teaspoon over the partially baked crust. Finish baking at 350 F. until golden brown. While still quite hot, cut into strips or squares.
>
> (Current Captivating Copper Country Cooking.)

Vast Recipe Changes

Desperation Pie, from the remains of ingredients from one's cupboard—eggless, milkless and perhaps also sugarless—were common for those who supported the war conservation through creative sweet baking. An almost reversal to the way recipes were baked before now occurred once again. If one was to produce any sweet-toothed treats, the use of molasses, mashed fruit and, of course, honey and maple syrup could provide sweetness, again as the early settlers had used. With World War I, improvised baking followed, with applesauce used in cakes to replace sugar and eggs, which were hard to come by. Corn syrup was used in place of sugar for bread, with shortening advocated rather than butter. Shortening replaced lard, also difficult to find.

According to Elizabeth Yetter:

> During World War I, food conservation was top priority for every homemaker in the United States. Sugar and wheat supplies were desperately needed by our allies in Europe and homemakers were encouraged to use less wheat and little to no sugar to make their breads. Corn syrup was used in place of sugar and shortening was used in place of fat during this time. This basic recipe for war bread gives modern measurements. The compressed yeast is replaced with active dry yeast. Recipe makes a very simple 1 loaf of white bread.

Although sugar was rationed, a well-known pie, chiffon, arrived in the early 1920s. According to Jean Anderson's American Century Cookbook, "These fluffy unbaked pies debuted in the early 1920s as 'soufflé' or 'gelatin' pies… Chiffon pies were invented by a professional baker who lived in Iowa, [by] beating egg whites with a fruit flavored syrup until light and fluffy… looking like a pile of chiffon."

Simple soul food and southern-style fare still have their presence in the Lake Michigan states, and sweet potato pie and pecan pie remain iconic American desserts.

An altogether different type of pie from the African American heritage was the bean pie: navy beans (cooked and mashed) with sweet and condensed milk, as well as various spices, usually vanilla and perhaps cinnamon, originating with the founder of the Nation of Islam, Elijah Muhammad. The recipe evolved because African American Muslims were encouraged to consume less rich foods. Today, this religious group sells bean pies for fundraising. Headquarters have been in Chicago since 1988.

BEAN PIE

2 cups navy beans (cooked)
4 eggs
1 14 ounce can evaporated milk
1 stick butter
1 teaspoon nutmeg
1 teaspoon cinnamon
2 tablespoons flour
2 cups sugar
2 tablespoons vanilla

Cook beans until soft. Preheat oven to 350 degrees. In electric blender, blend beans, butter, milk, eggs, nutmeg and flour about 2 minutes on medium speed. Pour mixture into a large mixing bowl. Add sugar and vanilla. Mix well. Pour into pie shells. Bake one hour, until golden brown. Makes 2 or 3 Bean Pies.

(www.muhammadspeaks.com/pie.html.)

> ### REFRIGERATOR COOKIES
>
> *Set Wilcolator at 400 (preheat oven)*
>
> *¾ cup butter*
> *1 cup granulated sugar*
> *4½ cup flour*
> *¾ cup butter substitute*
> *3 eggs*
> *1½ teaspoon soda*
> *1 cup brown sugar*
> *1 teaspoon cinnamon*
> *1 cup nutmeats*
> *½ teaspoon salt*
>
> *Mix in same manner as plain cookies. Pack the stiff dough into a mold or form into a roll about the size of a rolling pin. Wrap in waxed paper. Leave in the refrigerator over night. With a sharp knife slice thin as possible, lay on oiled cookie sheet. Bake 12 to 15 minutes.*

REFRIGERATOR CHANGES

Home refrigerators called for new recipes, such as icebox cookies and quickly made doughs. During the 1920s and 1930s, Wilcolator ovens and stoves had a recipe book promoting the use of its appliances. Chilled dough, or refrigerator cookies, was all the rage. Just ask Reddie Wilcolator.

MRS. RUBY STUTZMAN

Mrs. Ruby Stutzman, of Amish descent, has lived in the Nappanee, Indiana area for the last twenty-seven years. She is the mother of ten children and grandmother of sixty-seven. She has prepared a lot of food in her lifetime. Our meeting took place on a cool and breezy April morning at Ruby's lovely dining table, where she and her daughter-in-law, Rose, met with me and my mother. As we entered, I noticed a number of baked items on a nearby kitchen counter. Of course, I was hoping that we would be the recipients of those, and we were!

We enjoyed a vanilla tart pie made with sorghum molasses, sugar and egg. With the addition of flour, this mixture is stirred and baked inside Ruby's handmade pie crust. The result is a cakelike consistency inside a pie crust, delicious with the coffee and tea she served.

The Nappanee Country Store (groceries and small wares) en route to her home was a joint venture between her husband, son and daughter-in-law, Rose Stutzman. "The sign was special made for us, and the horse and buggy [on the sign] is our horse and buggy, duplicated from a photo the company took when we ordered it," said Mrs. Stutzman. The store reflects the Amish community's food requirements. The shelves had many ingredients for baking. The Stutzmans mentioned that many Amish women feel that the flour from New Rinkel (an Indiana Mill in business since 1846) is the best for cakes and pie crusts. Some baking ingredients on the shelves included New Rinkel flour as well as other flours, yeast, dried fruits and a delicious product called Amish Peanut Butter (peanut butter, marshmallow crème and corn

★ COOKIES ★

RICH COOKIES		PLAIN COOKIES		SAND TARTS
1 c. fat	1½ tsp. B. P.	¾ c. fat	2 tsp. B. P.	½ c. fat
1 c. sugar	1 tsp. flavoring	½ c. sugar	½ tsp. salt	1 c. light brown sugar
3 eggs	flour (to make	1 egg	¼ c. milk	1¾ c. flour
	stiff dough)	2 c. flour	flavoring	2 tsp. B. P.
				1 egg

Mix like butter cake—beat eggs whole—use flour sufficient to make dough that will roll out thin for crisp cookies—cut with cookie cutter—bake on greased cookie sheet 12 to 15 minutes. Cookie temperature 400°.

For sand tarts brush tops with white of egg, sprinkle evenly with sugar and cinnamon.

For drop cookies—use less flour and drop dough by teaspoon onto greased cookie sheet. These cookies will spread.

ICE BOX COOKIES
Set Wilcolator at 400°—Preheat Oven

¾ c. butter	1 c. granulated sugar	4½ c. flour
¾ c. butter substitute	3 eggs	1½ tsp. soda
1 c. brown sugar	1 tsp. cinnamon	1 c. nut meats
	½ tsp. salt	

Mix in same manner as plain cookies. Pack the stiff dough into a mold, or form into a roll about the size of a rolling pin. Wrap in waxed paper. Leave in the refrigerator over night. With a sharp knife slice as thin as possible, lay on an oiled cookie sheet. Bake 12 to 15 minutes.

OATMEAL COOKIES
Set Wilcolator at 400°—Preheat Oven

1 c. shortening	⅓ c. milk	1 c. raisins	¾ tsp. soda
1 c. sugar	2 c. flour	1 tsp. cinnamon	1 tsp. salt
2 eggs	2 c. rolled oats	1 tsp. cloves	

1—Cream shortening—add sugar—add eggs.
2—Add flour mixed with cinnamon, cloves, soda and salt, mix well.
3—Add rolled oats and raisins. If dough is not stiff enough to hold its shape add more rolled oats rather than flour to keep the consistency rough instead of smooth. Drop by teaspoon onto greased cookie sheet. Bake 12 to 15 minutes.

PASTRY

In making pastry it is essential to use:
1—A Standard brand of flour—either straight pastry or a blended flour.
2—A good quality of shortening.
3—Measure ingredients accurately.
4– Cold water from the faucet is used—ice water is not necessary—add enough liquid to hold mixture together—not enough to make it sticky.

Reddie Wilcolator cookbook for the gas stove, 1940s. *Author's collection.*

syrup). Amish butter is also sold here in the store. This butter is rolled in a log and wrapped in a waxed paper. Sometimes one can find this butter at farmers' markets in the middle states.

It is important to note that Mrs. Stutzman wrote the recipes that she has shared for this text by hand.

Mrs. Ruby Stutzman, Nappanee, Indiana

Q: Are the recipes you use for sweet baking "handed down"?
A: Since family is all married now, my cooking practice has changed from when they were growing up. Recipes provided today were used more frequently as most were quick, easy and less costly. Many were used at home while growing up and are handed down.

Q: Do you use local ingredients and products?
A: Most dry ingredients are bought locally. Fruit is raised or locally shipped in from a neighboring state. We raise many vegetables in our garden, too—corn, beans, carrots—and we freeze and can our harvest.

Q: Have your recipes changed to reflect new and different ingredients?
A: Yes, cream cheese, whipped topping, sour cream, etc., was not used before. We couldn't afford to buy it. Now some of the recipes we use require new and different ingredients.

Q: Is there other information or stories you would like to share to the readers about Amish recipes and Midwest ingredients?
A: Specialty baked sweets are served at Amish weddings: date pudding is a favorite. Amish weddings have attendance of eight hundred to one thousand. A noon or 12:30 p.m. meal is served for those that were at the service. 5:00 p.m. is for the cooks, friends that couldn't be there (as men that worked in factories, etc.) then 7:00 p.m. for immediate families and youth. [Another recipe written by Mrs. Stutzman, date pudding (see next page), is quick and easy.]

I remember simple sweets in the Depression. Sugar cookies by my grandmother. She moved from Oklahoma out of the Dust Bowl drought. They moved north in a box rail car. At times, the family owned chickens for eggs and, on occasion, a cow for milk. But it is easier now to purchase these items from the market.

Vanilla Tart Pie

This is a recipe from an old neighbor when I was a small girl. My grandma used to make this a lot, too. Most ingredients were available right at home. If you don't have sour milk, put 1 T. vinegar to your milk and let set a few minutes.

1 c. dark syrup
2 T. flour
1 egg
2 c. cold water
1 c. sugar
1 c. sour milk

Cook together until thickened, then cool and pour into 4 unbaked pie shells. Then combine the following and put on top of pie: 2 c. sugar, 2 eggs, 1 c. sour milk, ½ c. butter, 1 t. soda, 2½ c. flour. Bake at 400 degrees for first 5 minutes then reduce heat to 375 degrees until done. Drop the batter by Tablespoons on top of the syrup mixture.

Crust
1½ cups pastry flour
½ cup lard
¼ cup water
1 teaspoon salt

Place measured flour and salt in a bowl or on table. Make a well, or center in the middle of the flour and salt mixture. Take a fork or pastry cutter and blend in the lard, it will look lumpy. Add water, just until mixed. Do not over mix, the pastry will become tough. Chill until firm.

Spray pie pan with nonstick shortening. Flour working surface and roll dough into a circular shape to fit the pan. Roll to ½-in. thickness, allow dough to overhang pie plate, at first. Press dough into pan, and up onto the sides. Remove any air bubbles. Crimp edges of dough by hand or with fork tines. Chill until cool.

Preheat oven to 400 Fahrenheit. Using tinfoil line the top of the dough with the foil and use pie weights or uncooked beans to "weigh" down the crust. Bake for about 15 minutes, until edges are set. Remove foil and bake until crust is light brown.

Date Pudding
(A Favorite at Weddings)

350 Degrees
1 c. sugar, granulated or brown
2 T. shortening
½ cup dates, chopped or 1 c. raisins
1 c. milk
2 c. flour
4 t. baking powder
½ c. nutmeats

Mix together and put into greased baking dish. Pour the following boiled syrup (about 3 min.) over the batter and bake: 2 c. brown sugar, 2 c. boiling water, and 4 T. butter. Cool cut in bite size cubes and layer with whipped cream and serve.

Chapter 5

BAKING AND MILLING REACH THE MASSES, 1939-1945

WARTIME RESULTS

As many Americans joined the military, women took men's places in factories producing for the war effort. Six million females entered the workforce to build bombs, planes and tanks—just some of the equipment that helped win World War II. All Americans were urged to contribute and comply with the government's requests through broadcasted campaigns to help "Win the War." A wide range of products was rationed in order to prepare supplies and materials for the war effort. From tires and gasoline to rubber footwear and coffee, as supplies and demand were met, rationing ended. Specific food and ingredients that were important in sweet baking were also subject to rationing: sugar, canned milk, fat and some processed ingredients. Nonfood items that were rationed that would have affected consumer and professional bakeries included fuel, oil and stoves. Stamps were necessary to buy these rationed products. Nutritious and energy-promoting foods were considered "valuable" by consumers, and a black market was created for those in "demand" or for people who wanted more than was allotted. The president froze prices, wages and salaries, too.

In 1942, as World War II continued, culinary nationalism reigned. Food rationing controlled the supply and demand of food. But the prowar effort encouraged farmers to plant on as much land as possible.

The labor force was short in agriculture, and though farmers may have had an exemption from the draft, many still moved to the cities for jobs in factories. Between 1942 and 1946, prisoners of war were used for farm labor and logging, as well as in canneries. Overall, most Americans followed the campaigns for victory gardens (growing your own food helped families manage costs and availability), rationing and "living with less." A poster released by the Office of War Information noted simply, "Do with less so they'll have enough." And yet another pleaded, "Be patriotic, sign your country's pledge to save the food." On the whole, the American people were united in their efforts.

FOOD MESSAGES

Conserving was a message relayed from home to work, from the field and farm to the family table. Training sessions were available for homemakers to learn about living within the limits of the government food guidelines, preserving food at home and how to plan nutritious meals. Businesses also adjusted their products to reflect these national changes. Whether it was a magazine with recipes to hotels with "dance parties" to keep peoples' minds off the war, no one was left untouched.

Some might say that the messages about food were mixed. Eating for victory was composed of rationing on the homefront, growing victory gardens for food (but also as group support, to know that you were not alone in this struggle) and women (mostly) receiving government messages to feed nutritious foods. It is a wonder that sweet baking had a chance through such dramatic times.

IMMIGRATION

During the world wars and time between, Congress changed the policy for immigration. A quota system, partial to western and northern Europe, but quite limiting to southern and eastern Europe and barring many Asians from entry, was passed. It was interesting to see the movement of immigrants from the Caribbean and Central and South American, as well as Mexico. These groups moved freely into the United States.

INVENTIONS

By World War II, consumers had abandoned cast-iron stoves for the convenience of gas- or electric-heated stoves and ovens. The electric stove and electric mixer assisted in sweet baking at home, but the use of them stopped indefinitely as World War II began in 1939.

Mechanization since World War II replaced hand-cutting of sugar cane and harvesting beets, as well as planting. Large corporations dominated the sugar refining industry, mostly coastal cities. Commercial baking and milling equipment experienced nuances that propelled labor-intensive recipes and tasks into "quick" mass production.

Government began to take a more specific role in nutrition of the general public. In 1941, Dr. W. Henry Sebrell worked with manufacturers of breads and cereal grains to mix riboflavin, thiamin and niacin into their baked goods. The government responded with a mandate for the remainder of World War II: the federal Food and Drug Administration (FDA) ordered the enrichment of flour. "Incidents of malnutrition decreased for some two decades," according to the Answers.com website article on cereal grains.

SWEET BAKING INGREDIENTS DURING THE WAR

Cookbooks, magazines and pamphlets touted "eggless and milkless cakes" and stretching ingredients, as well as "new" boxed cake mixes. Rationing and wartime substitutions yielded new products from food manufacturers.

The most prevalent ingredient for sweet baked goods before this time was sugar, but now it was rationed. Sweet bakers, commercial and home bakers, had to think creatively! Honey, syrups and jellies were used to sweeten recipes. Fruit juice with gelatin, chocolate and factory-made marshmallows, along with puddings made from scratch or a box, could sweeten pies, cookies and many baked goods.

Feeding soldiers was an immense job, and the government once again, as it had in the Civil War and World War I, urged

---

SWANS DOWN EGGLESS CHOCOLATE CAKE

2 squares Baker's Unsweetened Chocolate
1 cup milk
1¾ cups sifted Swans Down Cake Flour
¾ teaspoon soda
¾ teaspoon salt
1 cup sugar
⅓ cup shortening
1 teaspoon vanilla

Combine chocolate and milk in top of double boiler and cook over rapidly boiling water 5 minutes, stirring occasionally. Blend with rotary egg beater; cool. Sift flour once, measure, add soda, salt and sugar and sift together three times. Cream shortening; add flour mixture, vanilla and chocolate mixture and stir until all flour is dampened. Then beat vigorously 1 minute. Bake in two greased and lightly floured 8-inch layer pans in moderate oven (375° F) 20 minutes, or until done.

EGGLESS COCOA CAKE
Substitute ¼ cup Baker's Breakfast Cocoa for chocolate. Sift cocoa with dry ingredients and add cold milk with vanilla.

ORANGE FROSTING
Combine 1½ cups sifted confectioners' sugar, 1½ teaspoons grated orange rind, 2 tablespoons lemon juice and dash of salt. Add 2 tablespoons hot melted butter or other shortening and beat vigorously 1 minute, adding more liquid, if necessary.

Who said 'No cake'?

No Eggs!

No Sugar!

No Shortening!

Swans Down says 'Wonderful cake... even with ration recipes!'

Swans Down
Cake Flour war
ration recipe.
Recipecurio.com.

companies to assist in this effort. Red Star Yeast, in Milwaukee, Wisconsin, contributed immensely to an important product for sweet and savory baking. "The company's scientific expertise played an important role in keeping soldiers fed and fighting during World War II. Shortly before the U.S. entered the war, the company began to develop active dry yeast with a moisture level of just 8 percent. Over the next four years, the company produced more than 5 million pounds of this new form of yeast to use in mobile Army kitchens overseas," according to the aforementioned cereal grains article.

The example recipe here from Swans Down Cake Flour, Igleheart Brothers, of Evansville, Indiana, exemplified the wartime rationing. Most Americans, including sweet bakeries, were directly touched by the shortages of food products in preparation of sweet baked goods.

Butter was labor-intensive but readily available; it was always a staple but was rationed during World War II. Butter now faced challenges with shortenings introduced to the market. As Americans became used to butter substitutions, like margarine, recipes and grocery items began to welcome this less expensive ingredient in keeping down family's food expenses.

Although Great Plains farmers produced an abundance of sugar beets, much of the sugar went from the processing plants to the munitions industry, where it was converted into alcohol for the making of smokeless powder. Soon, sugar supplies for consumers dwindled, and sugar bowls disappeared from restaurants.

PERIOD-SPECIFIC SWEET BAKED GOODS

From corner bakeries to assembly line bakeries, no one was exempt. Nabisco, headquartered in Chicago during the war, also altered its recipes due to ingredient rations. Companies like Hostess Brands, which manufactured Twinkies, had originally filled some of their cakes with banana cream. But now, due to rationing, Hostess switched to a vanilla cream, which has remained as its present popular filling.

The Wisconsin State Fair had been held every year since 1851 and had always showcased local foods and sweet baked goods. But according to the Original Cream Puffs website, "because of rationing during World War II, there was a shortage of whipping cream. In fact, the Dairy Bakery was closed in 1944, 1945, and 1946 due to the war. Many people missed being able to indulge themselves in their favorite whipped cream desserts. So when the bakery reopened in 1947, people were delighted

A Lloyd J. Harris Pie Company truck could carry 444 crust pies and 193 cream pies. The cream pies were stored in insulated and refrigerated compartments. The man standing next to the truck is holding a pie container in front of a bakery, 1940. *Wisconsin Historical Society.*

they could buy cream puffs at the fair again. And they did!" Illinois also followed suit with no fair during the years of 1942–45. The U.S. Army and Air Force used the fairgrounds for a supply depot.

One middle state company participating in the war effort developed the 1940 recipe for the Michigan-headquartered Kellogg's® Rice Krispies® Marshmallow Treats®. It was a popular "sweet treat" for sending to enlisted service people during World War II.

Rumford Baking Powder, part of the Terre Haute, Indiana Clabber Girl product line, distributed recipes reflecting the wartime rationing.

MRS. LILLIAN DEVRIES

The 4-H Club, which stand for "Heart, Health, Head and Hands," grew from rural America. Mrs. DeVries is an example of what belonging to 4-H involved.

"The history of 4-H is one of the most significant and far-reaching stories in America: a story of youth education, community pride and responsibility, personal leadership, and volunteerism. Truly unique—born at the grassroots level and involving special public-private partnerships at the local, state and national levels—it represents the very essence of America's growth. Over a century since it began, 4-H continues to thrive and expand today as one of America's foremost youth development initiatives. While constantly continuing to change in support of the evolving needs of young people today, most of the original concepts and philosophies—the proven strengths—remain unchanged," according to the 4-H preservation program website.

Wisconsin, like many states, held state and county fairs and festivals, originating in the late 1800s. These events showcased local ingredients, products and inventions. Miss Lillian Hendrickson (now DeVries) and Miss Evelyn Krinke (now Smith) were two young ladies involved in

RUMFORD HONEY CAKE

Any nutrition expert will tell you about honey's qualifications as a pure natural sweetening, and you'll find out that it helps a cake stay fresh longer.

2 cups sifted cake flour
3 teaspoons Rumford Baking Powder
¼ teaspoon salt
½ cup shortening
2 egg yolks
1 cup honey
½ cup milk
2 egg whites
1 teaspoon vanilla

SIFT together flour, Rumford Baking Powder and salt. Cream shortening until light. Beat egg yolks until lemon colored, gradually adding ½ cup of the honey while beating. Add the egg-honey mixture slowly to the creamed shortening, creaming while adding. Add sifted dry ingredients alternately with milk, mixing well after each addition. Beat egg whites until stiff; gradually beat in remaining ½ cup of honey until mixture stands in stiff peaks. Fold into cake batter until well-blended. Bake in 2 greased 9-inch layer cake pans in a moderate oven (375° F.) for 30 minutes. Cool and frost as desired.

(Recipe Curio. http://recipecurio.com/rumford-sugarless-recipes.)

The 1934 cake competition in Columbia County, Wisconsin, earned Mrs. Lillian Hendrickson (now Devries, left) and partner Miss Evelyn Krinke (now Smith) a blue ribbon. The same recipe took them to the Wisconsin Fair, where they also won a blue ribbon, baking both cakes on a hearth fire.

YELLOW SPONGE CAKE (CIRCA 1930S)

3 eggs
pinch of salt
1 cup sugar
2 teaspoons vinegar
3 teaspoons warm water
1 cup flour
2 teaspoons baking powder

Beat eggs separately. To yolks add sugar, water, salt and vinegar. Fold in whites, flour and baking powder, blending together; bake in cake pan in moderate oven for 20 minutes or until delicate and slightly brown.

the Welsh Prairie Livewires 4-H Club vying to win the cake baking competition in Columbia County Fair in Portage, Wisconsin. Their yellow sponge cake baked perfectly in the wood-burning oven, earning them a blue ribbon. The same recipe took them to the Wisconsin State Fair, where it also won a blue ribbon.

Mrs. DeVries and I met in a most unexpected way: by telephone. Blue ribbon winners and state fairs have always interested me. Finding someone who had won the blue ribbon, and especially during the 1930s, was going to be a challenge. Luckily, Lillian took a chance and decided to share her story.

Mrs. Lillian DeVries, Friesland, Wisconsin

Mrs. Hendrickson-DeVries still remembers "stoking and maintaining the oven fire—things were much different back then. So many years have gone by, its hard to remember." Mrs. Hendrickson-DeVries was one of nine children; dairy farming was what the family did, and a few still do today.

Q. What competition did you enter?
A. I was in high school in 1934 and entered the cake competition in Columbia County, Wisconsin.

Q. Category of the event?
A. We were 4-H Club representatives. We had a little song we sang in the beginning of our events.

Q. Why did you enter the contest?
A. I entered the contest for speaking and competition exposure.

Q. How did you select your recipe?
A. I had made this yellow sponge cake recipe for my family and thought it was good.

Q. How did you react when you won the prize?
A. We were very happy and surprised.

Q. Did you receive a blue ribbon?
A. We really received a blue ribbon but also received a letter with congratulations.

Q. Did you continue to bake this recipe for other people?
A. Over the years, I continued to bake this cake for family at home and guests.

Chapter 6

WOMEN AFTER THE WAR, 1945-1950s

THE MODERN-DAY CONSUMER

From hearth baking to conveyor belts, sweet baking was an all-day affair, typically managed by women at home in the 1800s and early 1900s. As World War II ended, women began spending more time at home again. Returning GIs from faraway places brought home requests for women to reproduce flavors from Europe and the Pacific—even Hawaiian-American food took a spotlight (think pineapple cake!). Americanized versions of lasagna, chop suey and the pupu platter from Polynesia might be completed by an instant tapioca dessert.

Contemporary magazines and cookbooks delegated complete menu suggestions for women to prepare for their families. Were all of the items from scratch? Not necessarily, but purchasing canned products and pouring it into boxed mixes at your home still constituted "homemade."

The last rationed item, sugar, became more widely available again in 1947. Sweet baking was back. The 1950s supermarkets began to dominate the retail food business. Supermarket chains began to have their own in-store bakeries.

"On May 22, 1946, the New Haven Restaurant Institute opened its doors in downtown New Haven, CT as the first and only school of its kind in the United States. Specifically created to train returning World War II veterans in the culinary arts, the Institute enrolled 50 students and employed a faculty consisting of a chef, a baker, and a dietitian," according to the Culinary Institute of America website.

Originally known as the New Haven Institute, what is today the culinary institute offered training to veterans in the varying culinary occupations, as well as offered a "formal" school setting, including certificates. The New Haven Institute joined a number of other Lake Michigan state programs offering training in the culinary arts and baking: Joliet Junior College (Joliet, Illinois, 1902), Milwaukee Area Technical College (Milwaukee, Wisconsin, 1911) and Washburne Culinary Institute (Chicago, Illinois, 1920s). American society saw a shift from a more traditional/old style "apprenticeship" (learning skills directly from the sweet baker) to employers who sought sweet bakers who had some training from professional programs. This shift was gradual and not necessarily noticed until the 1990s. Vocational/technical programs were the modern answer for some of the baking workforce.

Meanwhile, factory-prepared sweet baked goods continued forward. The "trained" sweet bakers and skilled artisans may never have seen a factory, but they may have been given an opportunity for supervisory jobs or jobs that designed and developed sweet bakery products with shelf stability! After the war, the state fairs that had ceased operations opened to the "hungry" public—hungry for not only sweet foods but also entertainment, celebrations and agricultural showcases, as they had once before. A change had occurred. "By the end of World War II, the nonagricultural side of the State Fair had grown," and "the interdependency of agriculture and industry" was stressed, according to the State of Michigan website.

> *Check Your Grocer's Shelves*
>
> *Today's packaged cake mixes produce superb cakes—high, light, tender and delicious—all with a great savings of time and work. When you go to market to pick up a mix, you'll find favorites like these:*
>
> *Snowy angel food*
> *Rich devil's food*
> *Spicy gingerbread*
> *Fragrant spice cake*
> *Fluffy white cake*
> *Golden yellow cake*
> *Marvel marble cake, etc.*
>
> *Once you have made your choice, just read, then follow to the letter, those one-two-three label directions. See how quickly you can whip up your cake by hand or with an electric mixer, pour batter into the pan or pans, and bake it. (Remember, it really is your cake, for you've baked it!)*
>
> (Good Housekeeping's Cake Book. *Chicago, IL: Consolidated Book Publishers, 1958.*)

Population Changes

After the war, Europeans began to immigrate to the United States. Europeans entered as refugees from a war-torn continent. Foreign-born brides of U.S. soldiers were also allowed to immigrate as "war brides." Jobs were plentiful, as most women who had worked for the war effort now returned back to the home. Germans, Canadians, Mexicans, Italians and immigrants from the UK were the predominant groups, 1,035,000 from 1941 to 1950. President Truman urged Congress to allow homeless war victims and displaced persons, direct effects of World War II, to enter the United States.

Operation Wetback returned thousands of illegal immigrants to Mexico in 1954, and the Hart Cellar Act in 1965 replaced immigration quotas but had an inclination to immigrants with preferred job skills and family relationships, as well as those with relatives already residing in the United States.

INVENTIONS AND INGREDIENTS

The 1950s saw freezers in many people's homes, changing the way food could be stored for sweet baking. Although the first microwave was available in 1954, the microwave has never been a strong tool for commercial or home baking production.

What about frozen desserts that are not ice cream? In the 1950s, the baking industry was revolutionized with new technology and also saw the development of frozen baked products. A process was developed for freezing desserts that maintained quality. Baking, freezing and distributing now happened in one foil pan. Or one could purchase the product, unbaked, and the consumer or the store (or bakeries) could bake the product on the premises or at home. This nuance not only allowed for extended storage in freezers but also enabled the producer to ship the frozen product—accessibility and affordability were passed on to the consumer. The first patent for rolled frozen pie crust dough, and the preparation of it, occurred in 1955.

Liquid fats were certainly not new to this era. Technically, melting butter or margarine constituted a liquid fat when warm, but as it cooled it solidified and changed the product. The invention of convenience mixes, liquid fats and reliable ovens allowed baking to become quite simple and quick. Powdered mixes for custards and gelatins (Jell-O and Knox) were available in 1830s, and the first powdered mix for pancakes, Aunt Jemima, was available in the 1890s. But cake mixes were looked on with suspicion at first, when all one might need to add was water.

Companies "working" on cake mixes had trials and errors in the beginning. The 1920s first saw cake mixes with varying ways to produce the batter, and the mixes were not always consistent. The year 1932 saw the first printed advertisement for a cake mix, by Dromedary. By the 1940s, many Midwest companies, including Swans Down Cake Flour in Indiana, had made cake making easy. Mixes with minimal ingredients added by the consumer yielded a cake made at home. But with the accessibility of cake mixes in a box, liquid fat was the easiest for the consumer. This new oil method for cake making had excellent results and tasted quite good.

After World War II, PET Milk developed nonfat dry milk far superior to what happened been developed earlier in the 1920s. Dry milk could be weighed, scaled and reconstituted in a bakery. As the milk industry progressed with safe and sanitary product, dry milk production began to fade.

BRANDING

Brand recognition has always been important. Often those companies that invented products would protect their rights through patents. Food and specifically sweet baking followed this tradition. We saw earlier the invention of Jell-O, a sweet dessert using gelatin, which was new and original. Quick puddings/custards followed and were also marketed by Kraft. Both commercial and home bakers used these fillings.

The "Kraft Oil Method" was marketed in the 1950s, as it was "so economical…so easy to measure… [it] blends right through the batter for wonderfully delicate cakes. And they stay so moist and rich to the final crumb!"

Cookbook pamphlets that I have researched from the 1950s emphasized the use of specific brands of equipment for sweet baking and cooking. Companies

20 Wonderful Cakes *made by the new* **KRAFT OIL METHOD**

CAKE BAKING GUIDE

Type of Cake	Oven Temperature	Approximate Time
Angel Food Cake	325F*	1 hour*
Sponge Cake	325F*	1 hour*
Chiffon Cake	325F*	1 hour*
Cup Cakes	375F	20-30 minutes
Fruit Cake	275F	2 to 5 hours
Layer Cake	350F-375F	25-30 minutes
Gingerbread	350F	40-45 minutes
Loaf Cake	325F-350F	50 minutes to 1 hour, 15 minutes

*These cakes may also be baked at 350F for 45-50 minutes.

NOTE: High altitudes require higher baking temperatures; consult the Home Service Department of your local electric utility company for this information.

Top: "20 Wonderful Cakes Made by the New Kraft Oil Method." *Kraft Foods.*

Bottom: Oven temperatures, 1950s. *Author's collection.*

offered optional training at an "institute" or store, as well as a recipe booklet that reinforced the customers' ease and use for their newfound equipment.

Electric ovens were invented in the late 1890s, but electricity was not available to everyone and the equipment was far from perfect. As the electric oven became more affordable and reliable in the 1920s and 1930s, they began to compete with gas ovens as a baking and cooking appliance in American households.

SWEET BAKING INGREDIENTS: FRUIT

The Michigan blueberry industry was developed due to the efforts of Dr. Stanley Johnson, who was looking for a profitable crop for Michigan's sandy, glacial soils. By 1950, there were about 2,200 acres of blueberries. Michigan was popular because of its bagged apples in the 1950s and was also the leading producer of slices for commercially prepared apple pies. Apples continue to be handpicked, usually by migrant workers, to prevent bruising.

Wisconsin's Cranberry School opened its doors in the late 1950s as an extension of the University of Wisconsin; the purpose was for educating growers about new pest management and production practices.

PERIOD-SPECIFIC SWEET BAKED GOODS

The 1950s found Americans eating and treating themselves to desserts and sweet baked products that reflected a new palate. Rationing and eating for the victory of war was over. Ingredients and recipes began to reveal a new era of plenty. Irma Rombauer's *The Joy of Cooking* listed such favorites: "Chocolate cake with white icing, Velvet Spice cake, Ice Cream with cherries, Apricot soufflé, Gold layer cake with caramel icing, Banana chocolate cake [and] Butterscotch Brownies."

Traditional boxed cakes met a nontraditional baking ingredient. Recipe developments using brand-name products offered consumers new and creative ways to satisfy the sweet tooth. A plain yellow cake could be transformed, at home, with the suggestions

LEMON LIME CAKE

1 box yellow cake mix, follow box directions for your desired shape and size of cake needed
1 box lime gelatin mix, follow box directions

Bake cake as directed. While cake is baking, prepare instant lime gelatin mixture according to package. Cool mixture but do not let mixture thicken. When cake is cooled, take a fork and make holes throughout the cake, about 1 inch apart. Spoon the lime gelatin mixture into the holes of the cake. Do not overpour, as the cake will become soggy. Chill for 2 to 3 hours, until gelatin is set. Frosting—optional.

by manufacturers. In doubt as to how best to use the product or ingredient? Have no fear, customer service was near. Corporations created personas ready to answer baking lovers' questions. Companies created a home-spun feel to their boxed products and baking ingredients.

Industrialized sweet products certainly still had a growing market. How could management be on another continent? How could every cookie be made fresh daily? Reliable automated assembly lines filled sweet baked orders. What about ingredients and product development being outsourced away from the original home plant? How would the little cakes made in Texas be the type that Wisconsin folk would like to eat?

It is debatable as to when cookie crust pies became mainstream. Cookies had been available for so many years, but it is supposed that crushed cookie companies, including graham cracker crumb companies, were thrilled to have their products affiliated with sweet baked products. In conjunction with the very dependable icebox came the icebox pies.

CHOCOLATE PEANUT BUTTER PIE

36 chocolate wafer cookie crumbs
6 tablespoons butter, melted
3 tablespoons brown sugar
6 ounces cream cheese
¾ cup confectioners' sugar
1¼ cups smooth peanut butter
1 tablespoon vanilla extract
2 cups heavy cream
1 ounce chocolate, for decorating, melted

CRUST
Combine wafer crumbs, butter and brown sugar. In a 9-in. pie pan or baking dish, press crumbs and bake until set in a 350° F oven, 8–10 minutes. Soften cream cheese and confectioners' sugar until fluffy. Beat in peanut butter and vanilla. Whip heavy cream until soft peaks form. Alternate whipped cream with peanut butter mixture until combined. Spoon filling into cooled crust. Freeze uncovered for 4 hours.

ROESER'S BAKERY, CHICAGO, ILLINOIS

In 1911, Howard Taft was the U.S. president, a rhubarb pie cost five cents, hydrogenated shortening was invented and Fannie Farmer (cookbook writer, educator, chef and exact measurement extraordinaire) produced *Catering for Special Occasions*. In 1911, there was also a young gentleman, single, in search of a bakery in Chicago, Illinois. John Roeser Sr. wanted something more than wholesale bread deliveries. He opened a shop on North Avenue in Chicago's Humboldt Park neighborhood. North Avenue, where the shop is still located one hundred years later, is an avenue of many stories. Originally a main thoroughfare going in and out of Chicago, before interstate roads, generations of families traveled this route to visit and tour and "live" the Chicago lifestyle. Roeser's Bakery is built near a magnificent stretch, Humboldt Park, 207 acres, a respite from inner city life and

Above: Roeser's Bakery, Chicago, Illinois, early 1900s. *Roeser's Bakery.*

Left: The Roeser family at the bakery: father, son and grandson. Chicago, Illinois, 1996. *Roeser's Bakery.*

one that was established in 1869. Today Roeser's is Chicago's oldest family-owned bakery maintaining its original location.

John Roeser III, the third-generation owner, was eager to share his bakery stories handed from father to son. Soon to manage will be grandson John Roeser IV. Roeser's Bakery sign lights up and can be seen from quite far away. When walking in the bakery, one cannot miss the contemporary wedding cake window displays. Round is passé—try square and multicolored! Photographs on the walls exhibit one hundred years of business, along with displays of cakes for all occasions. Of course, there are many selections of cookies, pastries and doughnuts, too. Sheet cakes, special shape cakes, ornaments, balloons and decorations, and not to mention homemade ice cream, can be had with one stop. The day I visited, three monkey cakes were being decorated in vibrant colors, and a number-shaped graduation cake for 2011. A glass box encased two chef coats by the front door. John Roeser III wore one when he assisted on two television events, Food Network's *Challenges* and *Ultimate Cake Off*. They were testaments to his still sharp cake making and decorating skills!

John Roeser III, CMB, Roeser's Bakery, Chicago, Illinois

Q. What brought your family to the Midwest?
A. John Sr. went from Germany to England (where he was a baker), wanted to go to Australia but joined a Swiss friend who had family in Chicago and came to the U.S. through Canada.

Q. What differs today for the customer when they visit Roeser's?
A. Roeser's was the only bakery in 72 blocks during the 1980s and early '90s. In the 1960s, there were twelve bakeries in eight blocks! Customer's expectations and needs are different now than one hundred years ago. A century ago, no one had refrigeration, and transportation was very localized. People came to the bakery every day, sometimes multiple times a day. Today it is a destination for a specific occasion. We now have a party store, which provides accessories for celebrations; it is two doors from the bakery, so when customers are waiting, they can look at items that can be purchased for their event.

Q. Is the bakery the same physically as it was when opened?
A. In 2001, we opened Roeser's Party Palace on the other side of the parking lot to provide customers with a one-stop shopping experience for their cards, piñatas, balloons, tableware, etc. In 1949, John Jr. acquired the space behind the bakery from the city when they tore down the el tracks that were there to provide for additional storage and garages.

Q. Have your customers changed over the years?
A. One hundred years ago, the neighborhood was comprised of mainly Germans and Scandinavians. In the '50s, there was a large influx of Mexicans and African Americans in this area. I know my customers and their culture and values, and the bakery has evolved with the community. The generations coming to the bakery now have a twenty-year spread and are larger families. Baby showers and birthdays give me more business than Christmas and Thanksgiving.

Q. Do you observe any new trends or changes in baking or sweet baking in the Midwest?
A. The Food Network television program has changed the style and volume of cake orders. Custom cakes have been busy and popular. Cakes used to be decorated with a standard ornament on top. Cakes today also have created opportunities for additional merchandise to be sold. Old staples like white bread, hard rolls and coffeecakes have given way to more individual items and more trendy items.

Q. Do you prepare any of the same recipes as when the bakery was opened?
A. Absolutely. Sponge cake, Danish and the like are the same recipes, but over the years, some ingredients have changed in regard to their makeup. A devil's food hot milk sponge cake has been the same formula for as long as anyone at the bakery can remember.

Q. Do you prepare recipes that reflect a Midwest baker's palate?
A. My recipes reflect the Latino community in this area. Tres Leches [three milk] cake is very popular. We also make a chocolate Tres Leches. I am sure no one else makes that one. It is not as "traditional," but customers like it.

Note: John Roeser's name is followed by the initials "CMB," Certified Master Baker. This most notable certification was earned by a written and practical exam, as well as by displaying his commercial and retail work experience to the Retail Bakers of America Association for a professional certificate.

Chapter 7

Ɲew Traditions, 1960-1980s

New Generations

The 1960s saw major social change. Nonconformist roles at home led to women beginning to seek employment in the workplace. Having less time at home, or perhaps deciding that they may not prepare all of the "family" meals as in previous generations, led to a shift toward "quick food." With ready-made baked goods from the grocer or the use of mixes for sweet baked products, the "corner bakery" was losing ground. Consumers no longer began to depend on their local bakeries.

A resurgence of French influence on cooking reigned from the White House, where the executive chef was French and the First Lady, Jacqueline Bouvier Kennedy, also had family ties to France. Classical French cuisine was the dominant culinary repertoire at White House events.

Julia Child (an American from California)—with a very impressionable cookbook, *Mastering the Art of French Cooking*—arrived on the scene bringing American cooks "back to baking with European classics." Her step-by-step approach in the book explained classical French cooking and baking. This cookbook allowed home food enthusiasts to embrace "foreign food" and classical baking and cooking in a most friendly and courteous manner.

Television programs, such as the *French Chef* series starring chef Julia Child, media and accessibility to world travel for many Americans opened a new culinary repertoire for some and reinforced the world's varying cuisines for others. Chocolate croissants, profiteroles (cream puffs) and mousse-filled cakes were accessible from sweet bakers in many metropolitan areas or at least could be "special ordered." Don't be fooled

CLAFOUTI (CHERRY FLAN)
Yield: servings for 6 to 8 people

The clafouti, which is traditional in the Limousin (French region) during cherry season, is peasant cooking for family meals, and it's and about as simple a dessert to make as you can imagine: a pancake batter poured over fruit in a fireproof dish and then baked in the oven. It looks like a tart and is usually eaten warm. (If you have no electric blender, work the eggs into the flour with a wooden spoon, gradually beat in the liquids and then strain the batter through a fine sieve.)

3 cups black cherries, pitted
1¼ cups milk
⅓ cup granulated sugar
3 eggs
1 Tb vanilla extract
⅛ teaspoon salt
⅔ cup all-purpose flour, sifted
an electric blender
a seven- to eight-cup lightly buttered fireproof baking dish or pyrex pie plate about 1½ inches deep
⅓ cup granulated sugar
powdered sugar in shaker

Preheat oven to 350 degrees. Use fresh black sweet cherries in season. Otherwise use drained, canned, pitted Bing cherries. Or frozen sweet cherries, thawed and drained. Place sugar, eggs and milk in your blender jar in the order in which they are listed. Cover and blend at top speed for 1 minute. Pour a ¼-inch layer of batter in the baking dish or pie plate. Set over a moderate heat for a minute or two until a film of batter has set in the bottom of the dish. Remove from heat. Spread the cherries over the batter and sprinkle on the sugar. Pour on the rest of the batter and smooth the surface with the back of a spoon. Place in middle position of preheated oven and bake for an hour. The clafouti is done when it has a puffed and browned, and a needle or knife plunged into the center comes out clean. Sprinkle top of clafouti with powdered sugar just before bringing it to the table.

(Beck, Simone, Louisette Bertholle and Julia Child. "Desserts and Cakes." Mastering the Art of French Cooking. New York: Alfred A Knopf, 1961.)

by these "sophisticated" sweet bakery products; most Americans were living a life of variety. Variety encompassed various places from which to purchase sweet baked goods, such as the bakery or the grocer, or they were made at home. Again, homemade also had variety. The consumer could purchase a cake mix and add a few ingredients of their own. Or they could purchase a package of raw cookie dough, slice and bake.

FLASHBACK

The 1970s exhibit cherries jubilee, refrigerator desserts and cereal cookies made easy, such as peanut butter cornflake clusters and s'mores cookie bars. Quick and convenient stores, as well as supermarkets, now began to sell sweet baked items prewrapped, with a visually enticing clear cellophane package. These products, which had traditionally been sold at bakeries, competed with the conveyor belt products sold at the neighborhood corner store. Fresh doughnuts and Long Johns with a coffee increasingly became mainstays for purchase at a convenience store or at the new franchise doughnut shops—fresh for the consumer but no longer produced at the local bakery. Products were now delivered from the bakery/plant and filling the shelves on a daily basis.

Grocers also began to install internal bakeries to prepare cakes for quick purchase. Serving warm cookies from conveyor belts initially lured customers in. A special-order cake at the grocer could also have a message written on the cake, just how the local bakery would have as well. Fresh baked sweets began to move out of the neighborhood bakery.

Inexpensive sweet baked goods lined the aisles; preservatives kept them shelf stable. How could fresh baked sweets stand a chance against always available, ready-made and preserved sweet baked goods? Because ingredients are shipped and processed year round, the sense of seasonality was and is lost. Peach cobbler pies were celebratory and seasonal items that brought farm folk together during harvests, and now pumpkin pie or cherry strudel might be had on any day of the year. Contemporary tastes, with the inventions of food preservation and shelf-stabilizing ingredients, allowed for accessibility but meant the possible loss of traditions affiliated with those foods.

The issue grew bigger than what meets the eye. In the 1980s, availability and skill sets for American baking personnel began to fall away. Soon, finding a person with the skills to produce bakery items at the local corner bakery (not factory made) began to grow increasingly difficult. It became necessary to reenter culinary and trade schools. Medieval guilds were the first formal groups to train sweet bakers in western Europe; apprenticeships reinforced the skills through hands-on experience. These traditions followed for centuries—a master taught the student and an apprentice learned the trade. Culinary training, via schools in the Lake Michigan states, began to offer programs with academic degrees. An Associate in Applied Science degree (AAS) certainly was not new in education, but it was new for the culinary and baking programs. These programs espoused hands-on baking and pastry skills, with internships and working in bakeries and pastry shops giving real experience to their graduates. After all, where had all the bakers gone? Especially as factories and

ALMOND SOUR CREAM CHEESECAKE

After being caught up in a whirlwind the past twenty years, with food fads and lifestyles changing faster than you can run a marathon, many people say that it is now time to take a breath, slow down and hark back to a simpler time in America…time to go back to basics.

Simplicity is cheesecake's only secret: feathery light or lusciously sweet and made of cream or cottage cheese or ricotta.

CRUST

1 package graham crackers, ground (2 cups)

½ cup blanched almonds—remove skins

⅓ cup sugar

8 tablespoons (1 stick) unsalted butter, at room temperature

FILLING TOPPING

1½ pounds cream cheese

8 ounces sour cream

½ cup sugar

1 tablespoon sugar

2½ teaspoons vanilla extract

2 tablespoons amaretto

2 teaspoons fresh lemon juice

½ cup slivered blanched almonds, toasted

½ teaspoon vanilla extract

1 teaspoon almond extract

2 tablespoons amaretto liqueur

3 eggs

Preheat the oven to 375 F.

Prepare the crust: Combine the cracker crumbs, almonds and sugar in food processor. Add the butter and process thoroughly. Press the mixture into an 8½-inch spring form pan, covering the bottom and reaching nearly halfway up the sides.

Prepare the filling: Combine the cream cheese, sugar, lemon juice, vanilla extract, almond extract and amaretto in the bowl of a food processor and cream thoroughly. Add the eggs and process until well blended. Pour the mixture into the prepared pan and bake until the cheesecake has just begun to crack, 45–50 minutes. Remove it from the oven and allow it to cool for several minutes. Reduce the oven heat to 350 F.

Prepare the topping: Stir the sour cream, sugar and amaretto together in a bowl and spoon the mixture over the cheesecake. Return the cheesecake to the oven and bake another 20 minutes. Sprinkle with toasted almonds and allow it to cool completely. 8–10 portions.

industrialized products took away the necessity to prepare products from scratch, the technical skills for sweet baking production began to diminish.

Cookbooks often reflect the era of what most people are looking for or desire. *The New Basics Cookbook*, by Julee Rosso and Sheila Lukins, showed us that the basics were needed for many of those cooks at home; baking skills especially would have been traditionally learned from home. Now those baking skills may be learned from a book. The cookbook guides one in preparing almond sour cream cheesecake, pear and ginger cobbler, black and white chocolate roll and lemon lace cookies—the lists go on. (Author Russo is also a Michigan native.)

Ever-Changing Immigration

National-origin quotas were abolished in 1965. The Immigration Nationality Act Amendments equalized immigration policies. The result was new immigration waves from non-European nations. The ethnic makeup shifted from a strong European dominance to the following countries, ranked in order of immigrants legally entering the United States: Mexico, Philippines, India and China.

The Immigration Reform and Control Act was passed in 1986, penalizing employers for hiring illegal immigrants. About 3 million immigrants already in the United States were given amnesty, mostly from Mexico. Would their sweet baking traditions affect American recipes now as other immigrant traditions had? Mexican Americans began to move from rural into more urban environments throughout the 1980s.

Inventions

Microwaves, food processors, convection ovens and Silpat mats (a silicone and fiberglass mat used for nonstick baking up to 500 degrees) were just a few inventions that made life more convenient and food quick and easy to prepare. With convenience came a noticeable reality: some people were not learning how to bake and cook at home! Industrial foods and baked goods were so convenient. What happened to small, independent bakeries? They began to disappear. But something was happening hundreds of miles away in Italy that was about to reflect what many countries, continents and states (like Indiana, Michigan, Wisconsin and Illinois) all had in common: food, including sweet baked goods, was about to get a new chance.

"A nonprofit member-supported association, Slow Food was founded in 1989 to counter the rise of fast food and fast life, the disappearance of local food traditions and people's dwindling interest in the food they eat, where it comes from, how it tastes and how our food choices affect the rest of the world," noted the organization's website.

This is not to say that all Americans had no interest in where and how they could change their eating habits before this Slow Food movement; rather, an awareness about their local and regional foodways was just beginning to resurface before this slow food movement took off. For some, the information about this movement was new; for others, it reinforced about how they were already living. The middle states also began to reflect on the bounty of their land as a new resurgence of eating and using "local" products ignited.

INGREDIENTS

Coffeecakes, cookies, brownies and cakes…frozen, thawed and ready to display and sell. From 1960 to 1980, the aisles grew bigger, with more competition from sweet baked companies lining the shelves. Manufacturers advertised to their sweet baking industry that low labor costs, unskilled pastry cooks and unreliable employees could affect the final bakery product. Small steps outside of rural America began to take place.

Urban gardens and farmers' markets began to rise in cities, suburbs and even downtown plazas—local ingredients, local people and even local sweet baked goods. Some sweet bakers began to display seasonal goods like blueberry pies, cherry muffins and strawberry cream cheese Danishes.

PERIOD-SPECIFIC SWEET BAKED GOODS

Selling pies on the roadside hardly seems to be a new innovation for the 1960s. But the Petritz family from Michigan had such success selling their cherry pies that they began to freeze them to keep up with sales. Industry improvements of freezers and mass production further propelled the frozen pie industry, especially for PET Milk, which eventually became Pet-Ritz. Frozen pie crusts now became acceptable to the grocery shopper. No-bake and quick-bake became niche markets created by Pet-Ritz.

Food manufacturers also began to offer frozen products to consumers that would have been only available to commercial bakeries in the past: puff pastry (think palmiers, French sugar spiral cookies; elephant ears; and cream-filled horns) and phyllo pastry (for strudel and baklava, a Greek dessert filled with nuts and honey). International and commercial sweet baking products were not yet mainstream but were still accessible to the food-loving public.

Some new and different sweet products represented versions of Mexican food, and some were just created for fun, like dessert chimichangas—rolled tortillas with a sweet filling, deep-fried and served with whip cream. Or churros, fried elongated doughnuts coated with cinnamon sugar or filled with jelly or cream. These were not necessarily all new but rather were versions of what some Americans might already have known about—doughnuts with different names and shapes. Custard in America, crème caramel in France and flan from many Latin nations were another example of similar desserts with different names.

CHEF/OWNER PAULA HANEY

Noted a *New York Times* editorial in 1902: "It is utterly insufficient (to eat pie only twice a week), as anyone who knows the secret of our strength as a nation and the foundation of our industrial supremacy must admit. Pie is the American synonym of prosperity, and its varying contents the calendar of the changing seasons. Pie is the food of the heroic. No pie-eating people can ever be permanently vanquished."

This quote is but one of the delightful aspects about Paula Haney's Hoosier Mama Pie Company. A Hoosier herself, with Indiana origins and a granddaughter and daughter in-law of farmers, Paula's sweet background entailed many years of dessert making for fine dining establishments. Her calling now is pie making at her own establishment, at 1618½ Chicago Avenue, Chicago, Illinois.

SPICE DROP COOKIES

This recipe uses the "spice" from peppers (Mexican origins) in the form of a powder. By adding the ancho chili, it reflects a trend toward spice in the American middle state palate.

2 ounces unsweetened chocolate
1 cup sugar
¼ cup vegetable oil
2 eggs, beaten
1 teaspoon vanilla extract
1 cup flour
¾ teaspoon baking powder
¼ teaspoon salt
½ cup confectioners' sugar
¼ teaspoon ancho chili powder

Melt the chocolate in the top of double boiler on stove; cool slightly. Combine eggs, sugar, oil and vanilla extract; whisk to combine. Stir in chocolate. Combine all dry ingredients, except powdered sugar, including ancho chili powder. Add chocolate mixture to flour/dry mixture. Stir until combined. Cover and refrigerate until chilled (about 2 hours).

Preheat oven to 350 F. Spread confectioners' sugar in bowl. Scoop chocolate mixture into walnut-sized balls and roll in the sugar. Place on parchment or greased baking sheet. Bake until edges are firm, about 10 minutes.

Hoosier Mama Pie Company shop sign, Chicago, Illinois, 2011. *Hoosier Mama Pie Company.*

SUGAR CREAM PIE (INDIANA ORIGINS)
Yield: 1 10-in. pie crust

CRUST

3 cups flour   *12 ounces (3 sticks) cold unsalted butter*
¼ teaspoon salt   *2 tablespoons sugar (optional)*

Combine the sugar, flour and salt in the bowl of an electric mixer. Using the paddle attachment, cut in butter on low speed until it is the size of small peas. Slowly pour in just enough water so that the dough comes together. Cover and refrigerate until firm.

FILLING

2 cups heavy cream   *2 tablespoons, all-purpose flour*
½ teaspoon vanilla extract   *½ cup sugar, brown (dark preferred)*
½ cup sugar, granulated

Meanwhile, prepare the filling. Whisk heavy cream and vanilla. Mix flour and sugars; remove any lumps from the ingredients. Combine dry and wet ingredients until thoroughly mixed. Pour into crust. Bake for 40 minutes or until pie is set or until the center is a little loose. Cool and serve.

Chef Paula Haney, Hoosier Mama Pies, Chicago, Illinois

"Pie should be local, picking what's local and making what you have right there," says Chef Paula Haney.

Because of Paula's great appreciation for pies, some are made from old recipes. Her shop has cookbooks (helpful in her pie crust ideas), pie plates and Depression glass plates that certainly can hold pies. A few tables and chairs give respite for those who need to refresh with a slice of pie and coffee. Sugar cream pie is an everyday staple on the menu at the bakery. It is also considered a native recipe to Indiana. In fact, it has origins from the exact same year Indiana became a state, 1816. Coincidence? We may never exactly know.

Hoosier Sugar Cream Pie, Desperation Pie and Finger Pie are probably one and the same. This pie's ingredients includes sugar (sometimes brown or maybe even maple sugar), creamed butter and cream with vanilla, and is prepared in different ways:

Desperation Pie = no eggs (occasionally 1 or 2 might be incorporated)
Finger Pie = stirred with your finger
Hoosier Sugar Cream Pie = originates from Indiana

How is it a pie? All of the above ingredients are mixed in a crust, resulting in a very sweet and satisfying pie! Ten to fifteen varieties are baked a day and sold at the counter, at Chicago's Green City Market and, of course, for orders online or over the telephone.

"A pie is very personal...very emotional and sentimental. Certain pies evoke specific memories for people," sighed Paula.

What is amazing and refreshing is that Paula works very deliberately to incorporate only *ingredients from the Midwest**, as well as seasonal ingredients, too. Rhubarb and strawberries were baked in the pies I saw on the racks one day. Of course, some customers have to *"stretch the rules."* Apple pie is sold all year long, and now her sweet pies also include a savory repertoire of chicken pot pies.

*Chef Haney reminded me that coconut and chocolate were two ingredients that everyone loves in a pie but that those—although delicious—are not sourced from the Midwest.

Chapter 8

A Sweet Melting Pot, 1990s-2011

Merging Foodways

"Indiana-based IndyBake Products and Illinois-based Brownie Products will be integrated into Kellogg's US snacks manufacturing network."
—Kellogg Company release, 2008, *kelloggcompany.com*

"Grupo Bimbo, the world's largest breadmaker, agreed to buy Sara Lee Corp.'s North American bakery business for $959 million to boost sales outside Mexico…Bimbo, which makes Entenmann's cakes, Thomas' English Muffins and Mrs. Baird's breads, gets most of its sales in Mexico."
—Carlos Manuel Rodriguez and Matthew Boyle,
"Bimbo Buys Sara Lee Bakery Unit," Bloomberg News

Mergers of companies in the Lake Michigan states is nothing new, neither regionally nor nationally. What we have been witnessing are global mergers, companies combining foodways through supermarkets, marketing or brand-new recipe inventions. Multipurpose food markets began to dominate in the 1990s followed by big box stores carrying everything from groceries to bicycles and doorknobs. Names that were traditionally "Middle America," like the Sara Lee Corporation, began to merge with nations and traditions that we may not entirely know or understand yet. History has observed that U.S. companies have continually merged and acquired products under one company name. Post was purchased by General Foods, Calumet Baking Powder by Kraft Foods and Swans Down Cake Flour by General Foods (eventually bought by the current-day Reilly Foods Company in Louisiana).

REAL OR CONTRIVED RECIPES?

Many food traditions and foodways are merging under one or several umbrella companies, yet recipe development may be outsourced, using products and ingredients that the chefs or food scientists know little about. Recipe developers may not be conscious of the cultural or geographic origins. Food distributors that represent food companies promise to market and sell the food manufacturers product. What does this mean? Well, food producers are left to the "ingenuity" of distribution and the way their products will be placed into the market. Recipe developers are given multiple food products and asked to produce recipes combining products, suggesting the ease of blending flavors and ingredients that had not been mixed before. Traditional and regional recipes may be crossed culturally with very different foodways. Will the original brands, recipes and traditions be lost? If marketing is successful, will this forced recipe selection be natural or contrived?

The twenty-first century finds many consumers conscious and inquisitive about what is in their food. Healthy, local produce and "locally" made products, including sweet baked items, have also created a growing demand for skilled bakers. From the 1990s to today, Lake Michigan states reflected the nation in its response to a growing industry that required trained baking and professional pastry chefs. Colleges and specialized baking programs seized the opportunity to meet these demands by offering certificate and diploma training (AAS and BAS).

Organic standards have pushed some farming and ingredients back to a time before corporate-owned agriculture. Consumers' pressure on the government gave rise to the National Organic Act in 1990. Specific guidelines and standards were required for products to be labeled "organic," and in return, a label was made to emboss on the packaging or products.

A resurgence of the love of "local" products has had many people open their eyes to the early indigenous crops that were once in the middle states—buckwheat, corn, sorghum and fruits—as well as the farming methods, raising animals and plants without using chemicals or hormones. To many of us growing up in the 1970s, apples meant Granny Smith and Red Delicious. Today there is a resurgence of growing heritage apple varieties, as well as other heritage fruits and plants, broadening

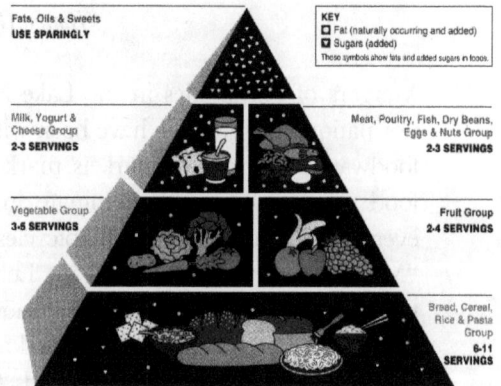

The USDA Food Pyramid, 1992.

the selection of flavors, plant varieties and tastes for sweet bakers. "Of some 6000 plus varieties of apples catalogued by the USDA from 1804–1904, only a mere handful makes its way into the hands of consumers today," according to Lynn Peemoeller's "Heritage Apples" article on the Edible Chicago website.

Demands for these foods also require skills to produce professional sweet baked products. Fresh, as opposed to manufactured, requires more work from farm to the table. Blending classic training with new local and indigenous flavors and ingredients results in the newest twenty-first-century sweet and savory palate. The involvement of the USDA in distributing and marketing dietary guidelines in 1992 certainly did not help the sweet bakery industry. The USDA Food Pyramid displayed oils and sweets to be the least desirable food group in an American's health-conscious diet. This pyramid was also incorporated into the educational programs for young American students. Would the sweet-toothed Americans change their behavior?

PATTERNS CHANGING

More immigrants entered the United States from 1991 to 2000 than at any other time since the 1900s—about 10–11 million, in fact. The waves of ethnic groups from Latin American countries are still growing, but growth has also come from India, China and Asia. By the early 1990s, more than 90 percent of Mexican Americans, as well as other Hispanics, were living in or near cities.

INVENTIONS

What inventions have occurred to affect our sweet baked foods? One is a machine that does not bake, ironically, but rather transmits information about many sweet baking recipes, ingredients and traditions—the computer. This revolutionary innovation can provide easy access to recipes and suggestions for baking, along with photos and how-to instructions. The palate of America has shifted again. Which immigrants' recipes transition into modern sweet baked goods is something that is always evolving and changing.

Another machine/invention that cannot bake by itself is also propagating an interest in sweet baking. The Food Network on television, established in 1993, hosts twenty-four-hours-per-day food competitions, demonstrations, celebrities and sweet baked recipes. Internet businesses sell ingredients and products that cross cultural foodways, too, like spicy cumin peanut butter cookies, which evoke a Thai satay dish with a peanut sauce.

Amazingly, cookbooks, food blogs and reality television shows immediately transmit culinary ideas, inventions and ingredients that we might not have been exposed to for years. Funky flavors and creations (think bacon and maple frosting, lollipop pops and sculpted cakes) leave many pastry chefs and bakers wondering where true food has gone? But on the other hand, we have also seen a resurgence and interest in sweet baking. Enrollment in culinary and professional certified programs is rising, all in the name of food.

The list of inventions that have made sweet baking more efficient in the last twenty years is long: blast chillers, silicone baking molds, infrared thermometers, food processors, self-baking and proofing ovens, automated jelly injectors and many more.

SWEET BAKING INGREDIENTS

"The bread and cake industry consumed approximately 75 percent of the flour milled in the United States. Other flour products included cookies, cereals, gravies, soups, whiskeys, and beers. Flour products were also used in nonfood applications… Approximately 85 percent of the flour used by industrial users was milled from hard and durum wheat varieties."
—"Flour and Other Grain Mill Products—Organization and Structure,"
allbusiness.com

Wheat continues to dominate the American palate, but agriculture continues to experiment with sweet ingredients: hybrids, genetically modified organisms and hydroponics. Sustainable food and energy-efficient food are ostensibly newer concepts. Natural ingredients grown without chemicals, sold and grown (and eaten) locally, are touted as more healthful for the body and the environment. A return to whole grains and "alternative/composite" flours has resulted in an expansion in the use of nonwheat and nongluten ingredients in sweet baked recipes. This book lists "composite flours" for just that reason—many consumers are looking to sample and experiment using grasses, beans, vegetable starches and nonwheat grains for their sweet baking.

While local and healthy may be "hip," the ready-made line of products for the consumer and home baker runs long, such as ready-made frostings, cake mixes and filling mixes. Ingredients for commercial mass/quick production include pre-tempered chocolate, sugar glazing machinery, additives, preservatives (extending shelf life), ready-made fresh-frozen bakery products and fats without flavors (like dehydrated cocoa butter).

Some traditions and foodways stay regional, like a Danish kringle from Wisconsin. Perhaps a fad for bacon, lettuce and tomato cupcakes will pass by. But some sweet baked recipes are here to stay, exemplifying American sweet baked traditions with standbys like brownies and chocolate chip cookies.

Period-Specific Sweet Baked Goods

Health issues are likely to affect products sold by the sweet baking industry. From the 1990s to the present day, food manufacturers, as well as bakeries, have been put in the spotlight to remove trans fats from the food formulas eaten by Americans. Already, labels are touting, "No trans fats."

Spices (nontraditional baking flavors like chili peppers, cumin and more), raw and unprocessed sweets, cupcakes, whole grain, gluten-free and, not to be forgotten, floral flavors in sweets (think lavender and rose) are the current trends in demand by consumers. Sweet bakers have been immersed in many of these trends as customers request menu changes. It is not to say that the "old" standards of cookies and cakes are passé, nor will the pumpkin pie at Thanksgiving be replaced by lavender cake; rather, the customer is king, and his or her food knowledge has been expanding through varying forms of media.

An extensive online survey was conducted by Wilton Enterprises, an industry leader in bakeware, cake decorating equipment, ingredients and classes for eighty-two years, located in Illinois. It also sells products on the Internet.

According to *Baking Buyer*'s April 2011 magazine, "We found that 75 percent of survey respondents reported baking the same or more than in previous years. One in four respondents view themselves as regular bakers, stating they bake a cake at least once a week. Cookies are the most popular homemade treats (82 percent)."

Somehow, through all of these inventions, changes and creative recipes, cultural traditions continue to shine through. Paczki (prounounced "poonch-kee"), a yeast fried doughnut with sweet fillings of Polish-American origins enjoyed on Shrove Tuesday, has made a comeback, with traditional flavors like apple to modern rosehip jam. This doughnut was prepared to use up the sugar, fat, eggs and fruit in the house before Lent began. Whoopie pies also reign strong in Lake Michigan state shops. Amish legends tell us that the two circular pieces of chocolate cake with a marshmallow cream filling occupied farmers' lunchboxes. They cried "Whoopie!" when they found this treat for lunch. When driving the Indiana countryside recently, it can be seen that Whoopie pies are still sold in local Amish bakeries, while urban coffee shops in the Lake Michigan states sell miniature white chocolate Whoopie cookies, too.

PUMPKIN WHOOPIE PIES

This recipe includes pumpkin, which makes it a more specific regional foodway for the Lake Michigan states. It is prepared in the same method, baked and assembled as the classic chocolate Whoopie. Pumpkin makes for a midwestern taste!

CAKES
Yield: 30 cakes

½ cup unbleached all-purpose flour
¼ cup buttermilk
1 teaspoon baking powder
¼ cup molasses
½ teaspoon baking soda
2 teaspoons ginger, grated
½ teaspoon salt
1 teaspoon ground cinnamon
1 can, 15 ounces canned pumpkin
¼ cup brown sugar
2 eggs
1 cup pastry flour
2 ounces unsalted butter

Preheat oven 400 degrees. Cream butter. Add pumpkin, eggs, buttermilk, molasses, ginger, cinnamon and brown sugar. Mix well. In a separate bowl, sift flours, baking powder, baking soda and salt.

Add dry ingredients to wet. Batter may be lumpy. Scoop batter with small ice cream scoop onto a pan with parchment paper. Bake 15–20 minutes, until they spring back lightly to your touch. Cool.

MARSHMALLOW FILLING (OR PURCHASE READY-MADE FILLING)
2 egg whites, room temperature
¾ cup light corn syrup
¼ warm water
1 tablespoon vanilla extract
½ cup granulated sugar

Using whip attachment in electric mixer, whip egg whites until stiff. In saucepan combine corn syrup, water and granulated sugar. Stir with spoon. Cook until softball stage (242 F). Begin beating egg whites while slowly streaming cooked sugar into eggs. Whip until cool.

Assemble pies by piping marshmallow between 2 cookies. Now they are a sandwich.

Chef Jacquy Pfeiffer, The French Pastry School, Chicago City Colleges.

Apple Cranberry Pie with Almond Crumble
By Chef Jacquy Pfeiffer
Co-Founder / Academic Dean for Student Affairs
of The French Pastry School

Importance of scaling: You will notice that our recipes are measured in grams. This is not only the traditional French way of measuring ingredients in pastry making, it is also the most common practice among pastry chefs in general. In pastry making, you have to be as exact as possible, as fluctuations in weight will drastically affect a recipe. Measuring every ingredient in grams, whether it is a solid or a liquid, allows you to do that even more so than with ounces. For example, the first recipe below calls for 4 grams of salt. That's equivalent to even less than one-fifth of an ounce! If you don't already have one, you can find a digital scale in many kitchen supply stores (or office supply stores), and they often measure in grams as well as ounces.

(continued on the next page)

Chef Jacquy Pfeiffer

The twenty-first century finds life moving quickly, food eaten faster and the ubiquitous "fast food." Quick often means processed food with little to no skill required from the sweet baker or pastry cook. The French Pastry School is a contemporary example of a program helping to prepare professionals entering and maintaining skills in the baking and sweet baking industry.

Chefs Jacquy Pfeiffer and Sébastien Canonne, MOF, founded The French Pastry School at City Colleges of Chicago with the mission to bring excellence and quality to the pastry industry through hands-on educational opportunities. The program was designed to meet the demand for persons to train in the art of pastry, cake and bread making. About one thousand students and pastry professionals total have participated in programs offered so far.

Chef Pfeiffer recounted his boyhood years helping his father in the family bakery in Alsace, France. In 1976, he began to bake professionally. Our discussion relayed how he arrived in the Midwest: "The Gulf War brought me to Chicago in 1991. After working in Hong Kong at the Hyatt Regency Hotel, I decided to find a pastry position in the United States. These were uncertain times…and chefs were hesitant to move from one job to another. Two jobs were available…I picked Chicago."

PÂTE À FONCER (PIE DOUGH)
Prepare the day before.

40 g water
12 g granulated sugar
4 g salt
150 g unsalted butter
8 g fresh egg yolk
200 g Pastry flour

Sift the flour. Combine the water, granulated sugar and salt in a bowl. In a mixer fitted with the paddle attachment, cream the butter until soft. Do not whip. Add the egg yolks to create an emulsion.

Add the water, sugar and sea salt mixture to the creamed butter. Add ¼ of the flour to this mixture. Do not over mix. Add the remaining flour. Do not over mix. Once the mixture is combined, shape into a flat square shape so it will be easier to roll out the next day and will save room in your refrigerator. Wrap the dough and refrigerate it overnight.

The next day, lightly grease the interior of your tart circle or pie tin with butter. Roll chilled dough out to 1/8-inch thick. Final size of rolled out dough should be 1 inch larger than the tart ring or pie tin.

Line an 8- or 9-inch tart ring or pie tin with the dough. Perforate the bottom of the dough with a fork. With a small paring knife, cut off the excess dough to give the pastry a clean edge. Place it in the cooler.

ALMOND AND FLEUR DE SEL CRUMBLE
Prepare the day before.

108 g unsalted butter
1.5 g Fleur de Sel
120 g American Almond powder with skin
108 g granulated sugar
108 g pastry flour
50 g American Almond crushed almonds with skin

Combine the first five ingredients in a mixer fitted with the paddle attachment. Mix slowly until desired size for streusel is achieved and add the crushed almonds. Spread the mixture on a baking sheet lined with a Silpat (or similar nonstick mat). Cover. Allow the streusel to rest in the cooler overnight. The next day, bake in a 325-degree oven for approximately 20–25 minutes. Once golden brown, remove from the oven. Break up the crumble to remove any large clumps. Allow the crumble to cool.

Sautéed Apples
Prepare the day of.

300 g apples, cut and diced
36 g unsalted butter
18 g Turbinado sugar (or light brown sugar as a substitute)
5 g Nielsen–Massey vanilla paste
fresh lemon juice from half a lemon
50 g dried cranberries

Sauté diced apples with the butter, Turbinado sugar and vanilla until golden brown. Do not over cook since this product will be baked again in the oven. Add the lemon juice and cranberries at the end of the cooking.

Remove from heat. Spread mixture on baking sheet lined with a Silpat (silicone mat). Let cool at room temperature.

Egg Wash
50 g Fresh eggs
10 g Fresh egg yolks
½ g salt

Combine the whole eggs, egg yolks and the sea salt. Pass the mixture through a fine strainer and store it in the cooler. Maximum shelf life is 2 to 3 days.

To Assemble
Remove prepared shell from cooler. Line prepared shell with cheesecloth and fill with plain uncooked rice. This will ensure your dough will not puff up during baking. Bake at 325 degrees for approximately 20 to 30 minutes. Once removed from oven, remove cheesecloth and rice and let cool for 5 minutes. Brush with egg wash. The egg wash will create a seal and prevent the baked dough from becoming soggy from the apple mixture. Add the apple/cranberry mixture to the baked pie shell. Be sure to pack in the mixture tightly and create a dome. Add the crumble, again packing on to ensure contents are secure. Bake at 325 degrees for approximately 15 to 20 minutes. Remove and let cool. Before serving, dust with powdered sugar.

THE
FRENCH PASTRY
SCHOOL
OF KENNEDY-KING COLLEGE

Chef Jacquy Pfeiffer, The French Pastry School, Chicago City Colleges

Q. What inspired you to open a school?
A. After working a few years in this country, I realized that there was a need for a school entirely dedicated to pastry because the skills for baking had faded and, in some areas, were practically lost. It is crucial for the future of the United States that culinary skills come back to the highest level if we want to be competitive in the future.

Q. When did you open the school?
A. Sixteen years ago, I built a teaching kitchen in a loft on the west side of Chicago and started to teach continuing education classes on the weekend and during the evenings. The school has evolved into a much larger operation located in downtown Chicago, Illinois, in coordination with City Colleges of Chicago.

Q. Do you observe any new trends or changes in sweet baking in the Midwest since opening your program?
A. Yes, great trends; when I came to the Midwest twenty years ago, meat and potatoes were king, and pastries were basically shortening cream-filled cakes. Many recipes were not made from scratch. From 1991 to 2000, it was all about creating sophisticated pastries and plated desserts. The TV Food Network started to pay attention to pastry chefs; some of it was gimmicky, but it put us on the map. Then the organic movement became increasingly stronger, and since then, the trend is all about going back to basics, working with the farmers, using natural and organic ingredients. I love it because this is what I know coming from France. It is about time that this country is reacting to this problem: overprocessed foods are too numerous, and they have little to no nutrition value.

Q. Is the Midwest sweet palate different than other United States regions?
A. Midwesterners definitely have a sweet tooth, and their taste buds always come back to the classics of pastry. The experimental molecular gastronomy does not have much room in the Midwest; we like real things that we can recognize.

Q. Do you prepare any recipes that reflect the Midwest sweet palate?
A. Where I come from is very much like the Midwest. We like apple, rhubarb and cherry tarts, chocolate cake, cookies and great bread.

Q. Would you like to share other information or stories about the Midwest?
A. The Midwest work ethic is strong. I have always been able to depend upon my kitchen staff, and now my students to come to work or class on time, and they work hard. It reminds me very much of Alsace, where I grew up; the weather is not always the best, so people concentrate on work. We like well-crafted things, we value hard work and the seasons are very important to us, as we create dishes based upon them.

FULL CIRCLE

What do you have a taste for? Chocolate chunky walnut brownies? Maple bourbon cupcakes? Jelly-filled doughnuts or blueberry streusel coffeecake?

Which immigrant recipes in the Lake Michigan states have evolved into our present-day foodways and modern sweet baked goods? The list of these recipes is long and varied. Every wave of immigrants brought food and recipes from the motherland, looking to re-create the "taste" from home. Every category in the contemporary recipe section of this text will have originated from at least one immigrant tradition: pies (Medieval origins), cookies (predominantly Dutch descent), scones (English, Scottish and Irish origins), crumbles and crisps (English origins), cakes (various European groups), coffeecakes (German and Austrian groups), pastries (western Europe) and fried doughs (the Pennsylvania Dutch in early America). Many of these recipes have developed to become Americanized or specifically midwestern sweets. The flavors and sweet baked repertoire evolved with the addition of natural ingredients, company ingredients, recipe changes, historical events, necessity and plain ingenuity.

There are only so many methods from which to prepare sweet baked goods. Some preparation methods require strong skills, albeit skills for handmade or factory-made products. Precision and consistency for sweet baked production, whether handmade or machine made, is key: measuring ingredients, mixing, proofing (for some with yeast), shaping, baking and decorating. All of these steps require knowledge and skills. Inventions and mechanization over the last 150 years of sweet baking have increased our capacity for production and technical recipe development. But it remains true that skilled pastry chefs and bakers are necessary to move these products forward.

Company mergers across continents make for a questionable future for our Lake Michigan state foodways. Will recipes, traditions and ingredients change or be lost through these business transactions? From home bakers to commercial sweet bakers, the results are coming out quick. There continues to be a demand for sweet baked products, whether from home, bakeries or supermarket shelves. Ingredients for production are sourced nationally for many commercial sweet bakers, whether by choice or not. But a return back to the farm and the "local" has shifted many people to come back to where the first middle state settlers began. Observe what is literally growing and being produced here, such as the grains and fruits. Necessity, inventions and creativity are how these Lake Michigan states began. It will be interesting to see where our next foodways take our sweet baked palate.

Part II
A Primer on Lake Michigan States
Sweet Baked Goods

Ingredients

Contemporary Glossary with
Middle State Culinary Origins

Flour

Flour is the most important ingredient in the sweet bake shop. Wheat flour (*Triticum aestivum*) specifically dominates the shelves and bins of commercial, retail and household bakers in the Midwest. The wheat plant is an annual grass and provides gluten, bulk and structure to most of the recipes—including cakes, cookies, pastries and sweet yeast breads. Home bakers typically rely on all-purpose flour, but the professional bake shop will have a variety of flours for various purposes. Each flour has specific qualities and characteristics.

Flour is made from either hard or soft wheat. Hard wheat contains greater amounts of proteins called glutenin and gliadin, which form gluten when the flour is moistened and mixed. Gluten is the elastic structure in dough. Soft wheat has a lower protein content and is best for cakes, cookies and pastries. Hard wheat is key for bread and sweet yeast breads.

Wheat Classifications

Six classes of wheat are grown in North America. Wheat is classified by the time of year planted, hardness and color.

Hard red winter wheat is grown in large quantities. It has moderately high protein and produces more gluten than other wheat. This wheat is excellent for yeast-leavened sweet goods. The red description refers to the color of the bran and layers of the wheat berry. Planted in the fall, Midwest states Kansas and Nebraska grow this wheat, but other predominant growers are Oklahoma and Texas. Hard red winter wheat grows until about five inches tall and becomes dormant with the onset of winter. It resumes growing the following spring and is harvested in late spring and early summer.

Hard red spring wheat has the highest protein content and is important in the composition of strong bread flours. Grown primarily in Minnesota, North and South Dakota, Montana and Idaho, it is planted in the spring and harvested late summer and early fall.

Hard white wheat is high in protein and is excellent for bread flours. This wheat is used especially in lighter-color wheat breads; it is not as strong in flavor as other wheats. The color is golden and has a sweet taste. Kansas, North Dakota and Colorado are the predominant growers.

Soft white wheat is low in protein and is used for crackers, cakes and pastries. Soft white wheat grows in Illinois, Missouri and Michigan.

Soft red winter wheat, also called Chicago wheat (because it has been traded predominantly at the Chicago Board of Trade commodities exchange), is low in protein and is used for cake and pastry flours. This wheat follows the growing pattern of the hard red winter. Illinois, Michigan and Indiana lead production in this wheat category.

Durum is the hardest of the six classes of wheat. It is used for pastas or in blends with other wheat for cakes and breads. Michigan, North Dakota, New York, Oregon and Washington are the predominant growers of this grain.

Milling Wheat

The wheat kernel is called the "wheat berry" and is composed of the germ, bran and endosperm. Once the wheat berries are cleaned and tempered (soaked to give them a common level of moisture), they are passed through the first steel rollers. The rollers are specifically designed to break the berry into the three aforementioned parts. As the berries pass through the rollers, the small pieces of endosperm are ground into varying grades of flour. The first "stream" of flour is known as *patent flour*; it has the most mineral content and can be compared to the example of the first crush of olives for olive oil—darker in color and thick. With each successive "stream," more mineral content is removed. Varying levels of streams are used for specific flour blends. The last and lowest flour grade has no bran or germ and is used in animal feed.

Once flour has been milled, varying items may be added and/or the flour whitened to give the ultimate "white and pure" look. The U.S. government mandates that "enriched" flours have small amounts of iron, niacin, thiamin and riboflavin added.

History shows that "white flour" was associated with the upper classes, and sometimes millers went to great lengths to whiten their flour, using chalk, ground lime and bone. Today's flour production has permissible additives of chlorine dioxide, benzoyl peroxide and chlorine gas. A controversial additive, potassium bromate, is considered by some to be carcinogenic. In California, the flour carries a warning label. When you purchase "un-bleached" flour, it is just that, not whitened with any chemicals.

Wheat Kernel/Wheat Berry Parts

The hard outer covering of the wheat kernel is the *bran*. In flour, you may see it as little brown flakes, but it is removed in the milling of white flour. Bran may be purchased separately in various grinds to add texture as well as nutrients to products.

The *germ* has a high fat content and usually becomes rancid quickly. It is the next seed to grow wheat. Germ is milled into whole wheat flour.

The *endosperm* is the largest part of the kernel, contributing protein, carbohydrates and minerals. Milled into white flour, this section is very starchy.

TYPES OF WHEAT FLOUR

When bakers buy flour, they look at two important numbers in the flour description: the protein and ash content. The ash content is an indicator of the flour's mineral content. This is measured by burning a sample of flour in a controlled environment. The starch and protein burn, but the minerals do not burn and are left as ash. The higher the ash, the darker the flour. Ash content for wheat flour will vary from 0.3 percent for white cake flour to 1.5 percent for whole wheat flour. The ash and protein contents, for this text, are approximate percentages.

Straight flour is milled from the entire endosperm. After the bran, germ and shorts are removed, the endosperm is cracked and sifted several times into different grades of flours. If the various grades are

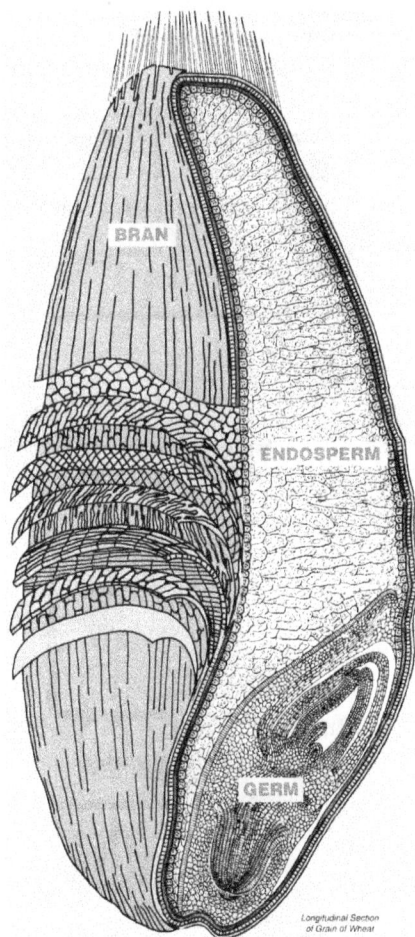

A diagram of wheat kernel parts used in baking. *Wbc.agr.mt.gov.*

recombined, you get straight flour. Straight flour is the darkest in color and is good for bread making—13 to 15 percent protein.

Patent flour is milled from the inner part of the endosperm. Made from hard wheat, it is excellent for bread making—11.00 to 13.00 percent protein, and 35.00 to 0.55 percent ash content.

High-gluten flour, as the name suggests, has strong gluten. Sometimes this flour is added to other weak gluten flours. Used alone, it is excellent for bagels, pizza dough and hard-crusted breads—14.0 percent protein and 0.5 percent ash content.

Cake flour is a low-gluten flour made from soft wheat. It has a smooth, silky texture and is pure white—8 percent protein and 3 percent ash content.

Pastry flour is a low-gluten flour, slightly stronger than cake flour. It has the creamy white color of patent flour and is not as pure white as cake flour—9.0 percent protein and 0.4 percent ash content.

Whole wheat has the entire wheat kernel included—bran, germ and endosperm. Because the entire germ, high in fat, is included, this particular flour can become rancid more quickly; 100 percent whole wheat can be heavy and dense, so white flour is often blended in—12 to 13 percent protein.

All-purpose flour is just that, slightly weaker than bread flour so it also can be used for more delicate baking. This flour is a blend of varying flour types by the mill. Regionally in the United States, southern all-purpose flour tends to be made from a soft winter wheat and has a very low protein content, whereas the blend for northeastern bakers will have a higher level of protein, as more bread baking occurs in this region at home—11.0 to 11.5 percent protein.

Self-rising flour is baking powder plus white flour, as well as salt sometimes. It is a great marketing tool, but it is difficult to gauge how much baking powder is in the flour. Therefore, preparing recipes with this flour could be challenging.

Bran flour has bran flakes added, coarse or fine, depending on the flour mill.

COMPOSITE FLOURS AND MEALS

The list of grains is plentiful, and they are added for variety and texture and for health reasons. Recent literature on health has stressed the importance of eating a variety of grains. Retail and commercial bakeries may carry specialty flours for specific sweet baked goods. In the United States, we tend to be a very wheat-based society, but there is a growing trend to offer sweet baked goods with more than just wheat flour. Meals are considered to be a coarse grain texture, merely a coarser blend of the flour.

Composite flours are a mix of grains, seeds and sometimes beans that are nutritious and functional. In sweet baking, wheat is often included in this blend for the vital gluten necessary for structure and texture. But for those who are gluten intolerant, composite blends are as numerous as there are ingredients. Whether the recipe is successful in texture, flavor and end product result is up to the individual, consumer and perhaps even the manufacturer.

The following is a list of grains, seeds or beans that can be used in contemporary sweet baking. The states listed are the predominant growers. Resurgence in small farming has also witnessed the demand for "alternative" baking ingredients, like those listed below.

Amaranth (*Amaranthus cruentus*) is an indigenous seed and plant that grows in the Americas; it was a staple food of the Aztecs and Incas. Amaranth was desired for its seed, as well as the leafy greens. The seed is filled with calcium, vitamin A and vitamin E and is rich with amino acids. Amaranth also has more protein than corn and rice. This plant is related to pigweed, which grows quickly and has a high fiber content. Perhaps not a newcomer to the Americas, it nevertheless has had a rebirth of significance for those desiring sweet baked goods that are gluten free. Missouri and Nebraska grow the majority of amaranth.

Buckwheat (*Fagopyrum esculentu*), a nutty brown grain, is not wheat, nor even a relative of wheat, but an annual related to rhubarb. The seed is so tiny, similar to the seeds found on strawberries. Buckwheat, when hulled, is cream colored. When roasted, the brown buckwheat (or kasha) gets its color from roasting. Used in commercial products for pancakes, breads and quick breads, half buckwheat and half whole wheat has almost eight essential amino acids (better than beef). Buckwheat is making a comeback as a product to mix with other flours. Brought by Europeans, it was prevalent in the eighteenth and nineteenth century but became less popular with the rise of corn and wheat fertilizers. Michigan, Wisconsin, Minnesota, Illinois, North Dakota, Pennsylvania and New York grow buckwheat.

Chickpea/Garbanzo (*Cicer arietinum*), a legume high in protein, calcium, fiber and iron, shows evidence of being grown in the Middle East 7,500 years ago. Four states in the United States, more or less, grow chickpeas. North Dakota and Iowa are leaders in the Midwest, and Washington and California grow it as well. Chickpeas are canned, dried or ground into flour. Chickpea flour has no gluten and is being used in alternative sweet baking, although it is already used in sweet baking and candy making in other countries.

Corn (Zea mays) is an indigenous grain in North America, developed by the Native Americans before the first settlers arrived. Americans, specifically in the Corn Belt—Nebraska, Iowa, Minnesota, Indiana, Missouri, Kansas, South Dakota, Ohio and Illinois—have further developed corn hybrids. The hybrid is referred to as "field dent corn." The corn kernel gets its name from the dent formed from moisture in the endosperm. Corn is ground in two different types of facilities. Cornmeal, found on many grocers' and bakers' shelves, is ground without the germ and hull, allowing for a long shelf life. Gristmills still mill the whole kernel. When milled with the germ, oils in the germ cause it to turn rancid more quickly. Cornmeal comes in various grinds: fine, medium and coarse. Corn flour, in the United States, is the most finely ground flour. In Europe, corn flour may contain cornstarch. Hominy is the dent corn kernel and is not used for sweet baking but rather in savory cooking. Masa Harina is ground dent corn; again, while not traditionally used in sweet baking, it has on occasion shown up in sweet recipes (like chocolate tamales).

Flax (Linum usitatissimum) is a grain whose seed is half filled with omega-3 oil. There are two different plants—one is edible flax, while the other flax is for clothing. Brought to North America in the seventeenth century by the French, the plant peaked in production during the two world wars as flax oil (linseed oil). The resurgence of flax is due overwhelmingly to the health benefits, nutrients and mineral content. Lacking gluten, flax contains alpha-linoleic acid, the essential amino acid needed from food. North Dakota and Minnesota are the predominant, if not almost exclusive, growers of this grain.

Kamut (Triticum polonicum) is a brand name for the grain variety Khorasan and is trademarked as Kamut (the supposed ancient word for wheat). A distant cousin to durum wheat, it was brought to America in 1949. Kamut is a distant cousin of Triticum wheat of the durum type, contains gluten and has a soft, buttery taste. It can be ground into flour and used just like wheat flour. Research dictates that the grain be grown mostly in Montana and in the upper Great Plains.

Millet (Panicum miliaceum) is believed to be the first cultivated grain by man. The variety used in North America, the pearl millet, can be ready for harvest in forty-five to sixty-five days. Gluten free, with a high protein content, it is oilier than wheat and is still making its way into contemporary sweet baking. This 5,500-year-old grain is cooked and served solely, ground into flour for flat breads and or used whole as "crunchy texture" in other breads, as well as mashed into porridge. When used in a yeast bread recipe, 25 percent of the mixture can be millet while still retaining a bread-like structure. Wisconsin, Minnesota and North and South Dakota are the nation's predominant growers.

Ingredients: Contemporary Glossary with Middle State Culinary Origins

Oats (Avena sativa) are harvested with their hulls or husks on, and once this hull is removed, the remaining berry is called a groat. Oats do not contain gluten, as wheat does, but oats do contain more protein than wheat. The groats look like brown rice, with a smooth, shiny surface, and is typically processed further into steel-cut oats, rolled oats, instant oats and oat flour. Oats make wonderful additions to sweet baked goods, either as flavor for the interior product or texture on the top in a streusel form. Oats, depending on the type used, can add a nutty flavor to a crunchy texture. Steel-cut oats (Irish oats, or referred to as pinhead oats by the Scottish) are passed through steel cutters that chop them into three or four pieces. Steaming the groats and flattening them with a roller makes rolled oats. They would be called old-fashioned or quick cooking oats if they are additionally steamed and partially cooked. Instant oats are steamed and cooked longer than rolled oats, losing nutrition as they are more processed. Oat flour is a byproduct of the flaking and cutting operations and is typically used in cereals and as an addition to breads. The Midwest in the twenty-first century ranks strong in the production of oats, but some farmers have switched to a more profitable soybean crop; in fact, only 5 percent of oat production is used for human consumption. Leading growers of oats in the states are Wisconsin, Iowa, Minnesota and South Dakota.

Potato (Solanum) flour is made from potatoes that have been cooked, dried and ground to a fine powder. This is not to be confused with potato starch flour, the starchy portion of the potato only. The flour is high in B vitamins, calcium, magnesium and fiber. Not traditionally used in sweet baked goods, it is gluten free and certainly can be used in baking. Potatoes are grown in all of the Midwest states.

Rice (Oryza sativa) is an annual plant second to corn in world production. The husk is removed and ground into flour. Long grain rice is best for flour. Other types of rice can be used for more glutinous applications, as well as for frying and thickening. Since the 1980s, in the United States rice flour has begun to take the place of wheat as any ingredient for celiac and special diet requirements. Rice has a mild flavor and does not overpower the overall taste of any sweet baked good. This flour is a good source of protein, calcium and thiamin. Florida, Arkansas, California, Missouri, Mississippi and Texas are the United States rice growers.

Rye (Secale cerale) is a grain used largely for breads. Rye is a grass grown for grain and forage. Rye, like winter wheat, begins growth in the fall and goes dormant in the winter, reappearing in the spring to finish its growth. Rye berries contain an endosperm, bran and germ. Rye contains more minerals than wheat but forms no gluten; 100 percent rye is very dense and therefore needs other wheat flours to give height and structure to the baked goods. Rye is usually mixed with 25 to 50 percent wheat flour for making bread and is only ground from the endosperm. Rye flour is also milled according to color and content, from strong to weak: rye meal (makes pumpernickel bread), dark rye, medium rye and light rye. Minnesota, Georgia and North and South Dakota currently grow the most rye.

Soybeans (Glycine max) are a complete protein low in carbohydrates. This bean originated in Asia and was brought from Europe to the United States, but not until the 1760s. Soybeans were used for industrial purposes and were not considered a food product until the 1920s. Like rice flour, soy flour is also mild in flavor, allowing for other flavor profiles to be tasted. Not widely cultivated until the 1950s in the United States, soybeans began to replace oats and wheat. The leading states for production are Iowa, Illinois and Minnesota.

Triticale (Triticale hexaploide) is a hybrid of rye and wheat dating back to 1875 in the United States. The experiment hoped for the hardiness of rye and the baking strengths of wheat. Triticale does have more protein than wheat, but it functions as bread between rye and wheat. Bakers recommend using wheat flour with triticale. Kansas, Washington, Texas and California are the leading producers.

Leavening Agents

Leavening, as related to baking, is the production or incorporation of gases in a baked product to increase volume and to produce shape and texture. Beating and creaming, two preparation methods used for sweet baked products, can incorporate air and volume. The baked product releases gases with a porous structure via air, steam, yeast, baking powder, baking soda, baker's ammonia and sometimes eggs. The temperature of products is something to think about: cool liquids have more oxygen, and liquids in an ingredient like butter create steam. All of your ingredients and procedures will give certain results when baking.

Yeast (Saccharomyces cerevisiae) is a strain from wild yeast that companies capture, grow and cultivate for the specific needs of the customers. *Fresh yeast*, also called compressed or cake yeast, is found in the refrigerated section of the grocer. Why? It is alive, perishable and can dry out and lose its strength. *Active dry yeast* is a live yeast strain that has been dried and needs to be "proofed" by dissolving the granules and exposing them to moisture. Although most of us follow a recipe, sometimes we will be without the yeast that the recipe calls for. A general rule is to use 40 percent by weight of active dry yeast for cake yeast. *Instant dry yeast* is a live yeast that has been dried but needs no proofing time; it is added as a dry ingredient and begins to produce gasses very quickly. *Rapid rise yeast* has been marketed for bakers in a hurry. Perhaps used more by home bakers, it is not typically used in commercial production. The yeast works quickly and

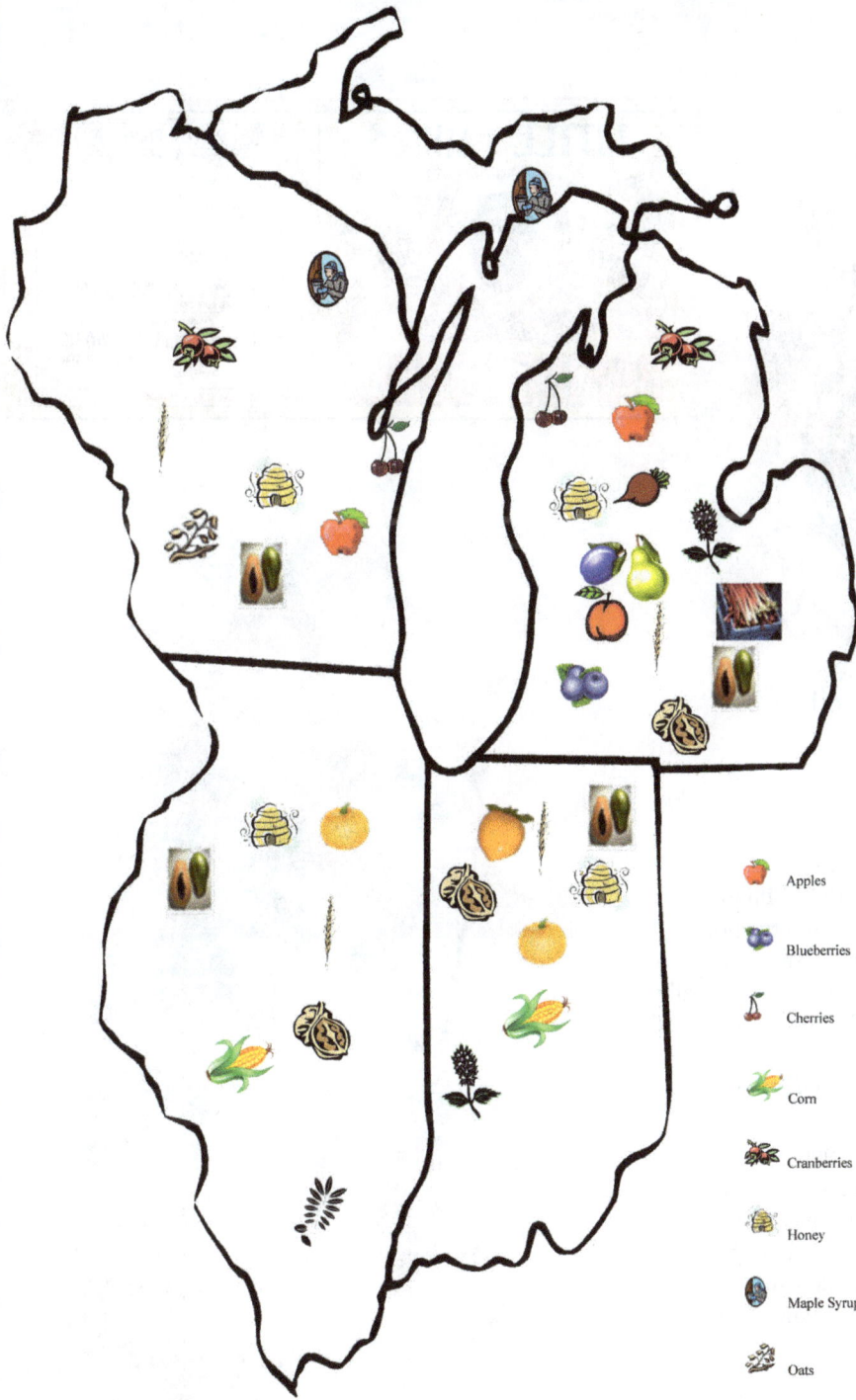

Map of Lake Michigan states' sweet baking natural ingredients. *Author's collection.*

Legend

Apples		Pear	
Blueberries		Pecans	
Cherries		Peppermint	
Corn		Persimmon	
Cranberries		Plum	
Honey		Pumpkins	
Maple Syrup		Rhubarb	
Oats		Sweet Beets	
Paw paw		Walnuts	
Peach		Wheat	

THE LEADING FLOUR

WASHBURN, CROSBY CO.
WASHBURN'S TRADE MARK
Gold MEDAL
MINNEAPOLIS

"We lead. Others follow."

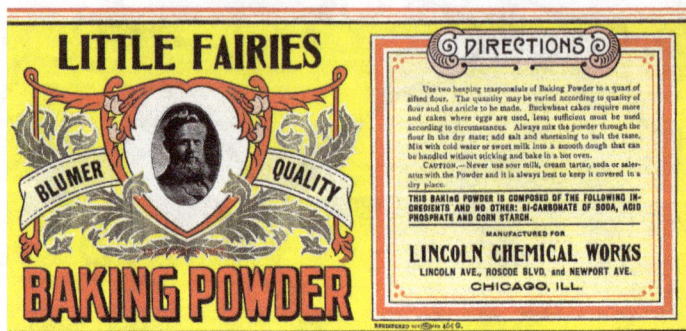

LITTLE FAIRIES

BLUMER QUALITY

BAKING POWDER

DIRECTIONS

Use two heaping teaspoonsful of Baking Powder to a quart of sifted flour. The quantity may be varied according to quality of flour and the article to be made. Buckwheat cakes require more and cakes where eggs are used, less; sufficient must be used according to circumstances. Always mix the powder through the flour in the dry state; add salt and shortening to suit the taste. Mix with cold water or sweet milk into a smooth dough that can be handled without sticking and bake in a hot oven.

Caution.—Never use sour milk, cream tartar, soda or saleratus with the Powder and it is always best to keep it covered in a dry place.

THIS BAKING POWDER IS COMPOSED OF THE FOLLOWING INGREDIENTS AND NO OTHER: BI-CARBONATE OF SODA, ACID PHOSPHATE AND CORN STARCH.

MANUFACTURED FOR

LINCOLN CHEMICAL WORKS

LINCOLN AVE., ROSCOE BLVD. and NEWPORT AVE.
CHICAGO, ILL.

Above, left: Washburn-Crosby Company advertisement from the late 1880s. Illinois congressman Robert Smith leased the power rights to flour mills on the Mississippi River. The Minneapolis Milling Company eventually became known as General Mills, with its award-winning Gold Medal Flour. *Wikimedia Commons, http://en.wikipedia.org/wiki/General_Mills.*

Above, right: The news in the 1900s was riddled with baking powder controversy. Manufacturers accused one another of using cheap alum or phosphate compounds rather than the expensive cream of tartar. Little Fairies was one among the many competitors vying for bakers' recipes. *Author's collection.*

Right: "Newman's Baking Powder and Soda Purity!" From Grand Rapids, Michigan. Due to the adulteration of food in the late 1800s, "pure and beautiful" images were used to portray companies' food products. *Author's collection.*

Pies are classic desserts that never fail to please. Fillings abound, depending on the ingredients and your palate. *Author's collection.*

Legend or lore? Whether baked in cups or with ingredients measured by the "cup full," these small cakes are delightful in bite sizes.

Originally prepared by using one pound of butter, flour, sugar and eggs, modernized recipes produce a myriad of flavors—such as the miniature lemon thyme pound cakes here. *Author's collection.*

Midwest ingredients and sweet baked products displayed on a mirror: dried Michigan cherries and blueberries from Three Sisters Garden, Illinois; fresh rolled oats; pecans; Morton Salt; and honey from the Chicago Honey Co-op. *Author's collection.*

Above: Parfaits are a simple layered dessert, with fruit, cake, custard, whip cream and more. Contemporary bakeries sometimes offer this sweet selection alongside their traditional baked goods.

Left: Springerle molds were first made in the German-speaking parts of Europe. Sixteenth-century molds were made from clay, eventually evolving into wood and metal. Immigrants brought their molds to the middle states, imprinted with varying images and using recipes that originally called for hartshorn (deer antlers) as a leavening agent. *From Chef Heidi Hedeker's collection.*

Although not 100 percent American in origin, the apple pie has become an iconic favorite. Early American cookbooks listed pie fillings to be savory and sweet.

WORLD'S FAIR

CHICAGO

1833 • A CENTURY OF PROGRESS • 1933
MAY 27TH to NOVEMBER 1ST
ADULTS 50¢   CHILDREN 25¢

The World's Fair Century of Progress in Chicago, Illinois, drew more than 47 million visitors. The Food and Drug Administration's presence reconfirmed a nation's concern about adulterated food—the 1906 Pure Food and Drug Act was still at the forefront of consumers' minds. New food inventions expanded ingredients for bakers. Kraft's kitchen in the Food Building at the fair included the Kraft Miracle Whip Machine. This "Miracle Whip" mayonnaise/salad dressing became a popular ingredient in cake making, sometimes replacing eggs, oil, milk and/or buttermilk.

dies quickly. *Regular instant yeast* can be used for many products but may not be useful for some sweet doughs; the extra added sugar burns itself out.

Baking soda is the chemical sodium bicarbonate. If an acid and moisture are present, the soda releases carbon dioxide gas that leavens the product. Heat is not necessary for this reaction, but the product needs to bake at once or the gasses will escape.

Baking powder is a mixture of baking soda plus one or more acids to react with it. Starch is also present to prevent lumping. No acid is necessary to use this product. *Single-acting powder* needs only moisture to release the gasses but must be baked immediately. *Double-acting powder* release some gas when cold but requires heat for the complete reaction.

Baking ammonia is a mixture of ammonium bicarbonate and ammonium carbonate. Only heat and moisture are necessary for it to work. Gasses are released very quickly, with little to no aftertaste, but it is best used in small baked products such as cookies, where the gasses subside quickly.

EGGS

Various parts of the egg in various forms are used in baking, like whole eggs, egg whites and egg yolks. Whether they are combined in a recipe batter or whisked with water as an egg wash on the exterior of a product to be baked, the egg is incredibly important. Eggs are most commonly sold in the shell. In the commercial baking industry, varying forms of eggs are sold: fresh and frozen egg yolks, fresh and frozen egg whites and dehydrated eggs. The Egg Products Inspection Act of 1970 requires the USDA to ensure that egg products are safe, wholesome and accurately labeled for the health of consumers. Egg plants that "break" eggs must submit to continuous government inspection. Egg pasteurization is currently enforced for all egg products in the United States. Egg products for the commercial baker are more varied than for the consumer. Before World War II, most egg farms had about 400 hens. By the 1960s, flocks of 100,000 were common, with a few locations having upward of 1 million laying hens.

Eggs perform the following functions in baking:

- structure—egg protein coagulates and gives structure.
- emulsifying of fats and liquids—natural emulsifiers help produce smooth batter, volume and texture.
- leavening—whisking eggs incorporates air, which expands when heated and helps in leavening.
- moisture—this flavorful liquid is part of the recipe.

- flavor—a higher yolk content will be richer in flavor.
- color—yolks impart a yellow color that becomes brown when baked and contributes to crust color.

Parts

air cell—an empty space located at the large end of the egg; it is located between the inner and outer shell membranes.

chalaza—a spiral, ropelike strand that anchors the yolk in the thick egg white. There are two chalazae anchoring each yolk, one on the top and one on the bottom.

germinal disc—a small, circular white spot (2–3mm across) on the surface of the yolk; it is where the sperm enters the egg. The nucleus of the egg is in the blastodisc.

shell—the hard, protective coating of the egg. It is semipermeable and lets gas exchange occur, but it keeps other substances from entering the egg. The shell is made of calcium carbonate.

albumin—the egg white.

yolk—the yellow, inner part of the egg, where the embryo will form. The yolk contains the food that will nourish the embryo as it grows.

In the United States, eggs are graded for quality by the USDA. There are three grades: AA, A and B. Grading indicates the firmness of the white and how the yolk "stands up" when broken onto a flat surface. AA eggs will be the most firm. In baking, clean and fresh eggs are more the priority, as most eggs will be incorporated into batters and doughs. Home recipes, which rarely indicate an egg size, use large eggs. Eggs are graded by size, indicating the approximate weight:

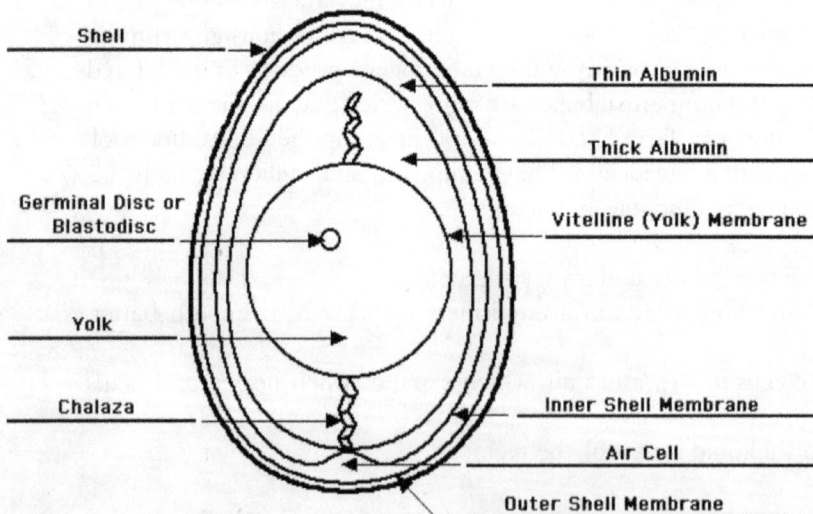

An egg diagram exhibiting the various parts used for baking. *Enchantedlearning.com.*

Size	U.S. weight
Jumbo	30 oz.
Extra Large	27 oz.
Large	24 oz.
Medium	21 oz.
Small	18 oz.
Pewee	15 oz.

Note: minimum weight per dozen.

THICKENERS

In baking sauces, puddings and fillings, many ingredients can thicken mousses and creams. These thickeners may be used lightly to thicken sauces and mixtures or in more strength to "set" a product for slicing.

Agar-agar derives from a plant source, red algae. Newer to the western market but used in Asia for desserts and some of Europe as a protein, it is sold in flakes, sheets and powder forms. Because it is not an animal product, it can be used by vegetarians as well as for those with animal dietary restrictions. It is dissolved in warm water or a liquid. When the liquid cools or a significant amount of agar is sprinkled on the liquid, it becomes solid and will then need to be warmed (softened) in the liquid.

Arrowroot was a plant that European settlers and explorers discovered in the New World. The tuberous rhizome was highly starchy and nutritious. It also had medicinal values. The tuber, aru-aru, evolved into our present-day arrowroot, as wounds inflicted by poisonous arrows healed with the application of the arrowroot. Arrowroot thickens at a lower temperature than flour or cornstarch and has a more neutral flavor, but it becomes slimy when mixed with dairy.

Cornstarch, certainly an American product, has been produced since the 1840s. The white powder, taken from the endosperm of the corn plant, needs the addition of a liquid and heat. In order to have a "clean" taste and feeling in one's mouth, tasting the product or ensuring that the white liquid is thoroughly cooked through is critical to its success.

Gelatin, extracted from connective animal tissues, is a water-soluble protein. Gelatin is available in powder and sheet forms. It is dissolved in warm water or a liquid. When the liquid cools or a significant amount of powder is sprinkled on the liquid, it becomes solid and will then need to be warmed (softened) in the liquid.

Tapioca is from the root of the cassava, also indigenous to the Americas. Tapioca is processed, producing pearls, flakes and seeds—pearls being the more commonly used form in culinary and baking. Because tapioca was easy to digest, a pudding was prepared and often prescribed in nineteenth-century America for the young, old and sick.

Pectin, originally derived from the cells of plants by a French inventor in the 1800s, continues its traditional use as a thickener in jellies, jams and preserves for baking. Research has also found it to be a stabilizer and a source of dietary fiber.

FATS

Fat has various functions in sweet baking:

- adds a rich and creamy flavor.
- tenderizes and softens the texture.
- assists in leavening when creamed.
- provides flaky texture.
- gives moisture, which enhances the shelf-life.

Many fats are available to the sweet baker. Each fat has different properties that make it suitable for different purposes. Sometimes fats may be substituted for one another, but this takes experience and experimentation. Flavor, texture and the finished product could be different when substituting fats.

Butter

Butter made in the United States consists of 80 percent fat, 15 percent water and about 5 percent milk solids. Butter is graded according to the U.S. Department of Agriculture: AA, A, B and C. Most bakeries use AA and A, as the flavor and color are consistent. Available unsalted or salted, butter that is unsalted has a sweeter taste and is preferred in sweet baking, as butter melts in the mouth. After eating pastries and icings, the mouth feels smooth and pleasant. (Twenty-one pounds of whole milk equals one pound of butter.)

Shortenings

Shortenings are made from animal fats, vegetable oils or both. During manufacturing, fats are hydrogenated. The process turns liquid oils into solid fats. Two types of shortenings are currently available: regular and emulsified.

Ingredients: Contemporary Glossary with Middle State Culinary Origins

Regular shortening has a waxy and tough texture and can be manufactured to varying degree of hardness for different purposes. This product creams easily, which means that air can be incorporated readily. This produces flaky baked goods and is used predominantly by home bakers and commercial bakeries.

Emulsified shortening is soft and spreadable and quickly coats ingredients. Because it is emulsified, it can hold larger quantities of liquid and sugar compare to regular shortening. When the weight of sugar is greater than flour, this particular shortening works well. Available to commercial kitchens, large bakeries might select this as a fat for their recipes.

Margarine/pastry margarine is more elastic but is tough and waxy. It is formulated for doughs that form layers, such as in Danishes and puff pastry doughs. Margarine is manufactured from various hydrogenated vegetable and animal fats, plus flavoring ingredients, emulsifiers, coloring agents and other ingredients. It contains 80–85 percent fat, 10 to 15 percent moisture and about 5 percent salt, milk solids and other ingredients. Some consider it an imitation butter.

Baker's margarines have a good creaming ability and are soft; they are used in various products. Unlike margarines sold by retail grocers, baker's margarines are made differently and are for different purposes.

Oils

Oil is a liquid fat and spreads throughout the product quickly, shortening the gluten strands (as opposed to lengthening the gluten strands with other fats). Oil as an ingredient has taken a new turn in the sweet baking industry. Quick breads, which often have a short baking time, sometimes have oil as the fat. A contemporary recipe change is the addition of a nontraditional oil like olive oil (heart healthy) as a "different" type of oil that may have been used for savory recipes in the past but now is used for sweet baking. Vegetable oils (excluding corn oil, as it is too heavy and overpowers the flavor) also work well as the "fat" ingredient for quick breads.

Lard

Lard, the rendered fat of hogs, is the ingredient of an era gone by. Once prevalent in the preparation of a flaky pie crust, it has been replaced in all bakeries by more modern shortenings. Of course, health issues also played into the negative effects of this product.

Milk and Milk Products

Milk

Milk, next to water, is one of the most important liquids in the bake shop. The development of gluten (elasticity in dough) takes place with the addition of a liquid. Milk is 88 to 91 percent water—the catalyst in beginning the gluten action. Milk also contributes to color, texture, flavor and crust, as well as nutritional value. In the United States, the milk is both pasteurized (heated to kill disease-producing bacteria) and homogenized (processed so the cream doesn't separate). Rarely does a professional bake shop use *skim milk* or *nonfat fresh milk*. Genetics, artificial insemination and efficient machinery have changed the dairy industry. The twenty-first century sees an overabundance of dairy cows and a reduction in milk consumption but an increase in cheese consumption. Dairy farmers are leaving a once viable industry.

Fermented Milk Products

Buttermilk is fresh milk that has been soured by bacteria. *Cultured buttermilk* is labeled as to distinguish from the original buttermilk, which was the liquid left after butter making.

Yogurt is custard-like milk that is cultured by a special bacteria. Some yogurts are flavored and sweetened.

Sour cream has been cultured or fermented by adding a lactic acid bacteria. The flavor is thick and slightly tangy.

Dried Milk

Nonfat dry milk (also known as nonfat milk solid), in professional bake shops, is skim milk that has been dried to a powder. In a recipe, this product is usually weighed in dried form, and the liquid is then incorporated separately.

Dried whole milk is whole milk that has been dried to a powder. The high butterfat gives way to the possibility of it becoming rancid. Storage in a cool place is important.

Cream

Half-and-half, according to professional bake shops, has a fat content of 10 to 12 percent, too low for it to be called a cream. But it is used in custard-type desserts.

Ingredients: Contemporary Glossary with Middle State Culinary Origins

Whipping cream has a fat content of 30–40 percent. In this category, there are also *light whipping creams* (30–35 percent) and *heavy whipping creams* (36–40 percent). Pasteurization is mandatory in the United States, but a label saying "ultrapasteurized" keeps longer, although it may have stabilizers in it.

Crème fraiche is a cultured heavy cream that is slightly aged. This product is thick but slightly tangy. It is often mixed into doughs, batters, fillings and creams in the bake shop.

Light cream, otherwise known as coffee cream, contains 16–22 percent fat. This is hardly used in professional sweet bake shops, but the use of it in some special recipes is not ruled out.

Condensed and Evaporated Milk

Condensed milk is milk with 60 percent of the water removed, with the addition of lots of sugar.

Evaporated milk is milk with 60 percent of the water removed, but then it is sterilized and canned.

CHEESE

The use of cheese in a bake shop may vary by region and bake shop recipes. But these are the predominant cheeses.

Ricotta in the United States is from cow's milk, and in Italy it is prepared from sheep or water buffalo and only sometimes from cow or goat. It is smooth and somewhat dry; the curds can range from small to large. Originally, it was made from the whey. This also is a cheese used for fillings.

Mascarpone is a "fresh" cheese with an expiration date. It is best used after it is made. Originating from Italy, mascarpone has traveled to the United States, where stories on origins and dates vary. Mascarpone is a soft cheese, and it is tangier than American cream cheese. This fresh cheese is prepared by American companies for not only sweet recipes but savory ones as well. Typically used for fillings, it is made from cows' milk. The butterfat content, 70–75 percent, is the closest amount of fat to butter.

Baker's cheese is un-aged, low in fat, soft and dry.

Cream cheese is soft, un-aged and has a higher fat content. USDA law requires 33 percent fat and no more than 55 percent water. Low-fat varieties do exist and have different standards.

NUTS

Black Walnut (Juglans nigra)

While other trees are grown in orchards in many parts of the world, the best black walnuts still grow wild and are hand-harvested in the heart of America. Every fall, people in the Midwest and east-central United States gather the wild black walnuts by hand from their lawns and pastures and sell them to local buyers, making the American black walnut an integral piece of Midwest culture.

Also known as the American walnut, the nuts from this tree have been used for both food and medicine. Two pounds of unshelled black walnuts found in the wild will yield about a cup full of nutmeats. This taste sensation made its way into the baking, candy and the ice cream industries, its rich accents complementing the flavor and texture of ice cream. The black walnut harvest is one of the few crops still picked by hand.

"Black John Cake has two cake layers made from dough that blends brown sugar, molasses, eggs, butter, flour, ginger, cinnamon, buttermilk, and baking soda and has a filling accented by raisins, coconut, and black walnut," wrote Evan Jones in *American Food*.

Hickory Nut (Carya spp.)

The hickory nut, prevalent in the Midwest, shares the reputation with the walnut and pecan as having a shell very tough to crack, defying ordinary nutcrackers. Gathered in the fall, this nut is known for its earthy, woodsy flavor and can be frozen and used year round for recipes. Hickory nutmeats are rarely found on grocer shelves, but they can be purchased through local farmers' markets or specialty mail-order stores.

Pecan (Carya illinoinensis)

Native to North America and related to the walnut, fur traders brought the pecan to the Atlantic coast from Illinois, calling them Illinois nuts, which accounts for the Latin name *Illinoinesis*. "Pecan" comes from Algonquin Indian word "pacane," meaning "a nut so hard it had to be cracked with a stone." Pecans are ideal for baking due to their versatility; full, sweet flavor; crunchy texture; and appearance. Pecans became popular in the South with soul food creations like pecan pie. This popular pie recipe made its way into the Midwest following the immigration north after the Civil War.

In the United States, the pecans are second in popularity only to peanuts (not really a nut), and this country produces about 80 percent of the world's pecans. Pecans come in a variety of sizes, and there are in excess of one thousand varieties of pecans.

FRUITS IN THE LAKE MICHIGAN STATES

There are only three *major* fruits native to North America—cranberries, blueberries and Concord grapes. However, there are many more *minor* indigenous fruits native to certain regions of the United States that are popular within specific regions of the Midwest.

While many indigenous fruits such as the persimmon and pawpaw have potential for commercial development, several negative factors prevent them from becoming commercial crops. For example, the pawpaw fruit deteriorates rapidly after ripening, is highly variable in size (ranging anywhere from four to seventeen ounces), has a lot of seeds and varies in sweetness; perhaps the biggest roadblock is that the trees will not fruit before they reach five years of age. For the persimmon, it was found that the Asian variety was more suited to commercial production than the American persimmon because its production time is more widespread than the American variety. Therefore, these two native fruits tend to rely on local farmers' markets, unlike other native fruits, such as the cranberry, which has become popularized enough for commercial production.

Apples (Rosaceae spp.)

Apple recipes in sweet baking are plentiful, but it is duly noted this fruit was *not* indigenous to the United States. Only the crabapple is indigenous to North America. The Pilgrims brought the apple to America, whereupon legend and truth has it that John Chapman (Johnny Appleseed) walked across America, sowing apple seeds. He is thought to have planted ten thousand acres worth of orchards. Located a few miles northwest of Grand Rapids, Michigan, is an area known as the Fruit Ridge. Apples are Michigan's largest and most valuable fruit crop. On average, Michigan harvests about 20 million bushels (800 million pounds) of apples per year. Michigan is the nation's third-largest producer of apples, with 950 apple growers living and working by Lake Michigan. Small family farmers who operate their own orchards dominate the Michigan apple industry. About 63 percent of the apple crop is typically eaten as fresh fruit, while about 36 percent is processed into apple products (juice, cider, dried, frozen and canned). Other uses include the making of baby food, apple butter or jelly and vinegar.

Apricots (Prunus armeniaca)

Planted by Spaniards in the United States, the British tried unsuccessfully to cultivate this fruit tree. The Midwest needs an apricot able to survive some below zero winters.

Blueberries (Vaccinium corymbosum)

Michigan is the number one state for highbush blueberry production. Harvested from June to October, with July being the peak month for production, there are more than 60 million pounds being grown in Michigan each year. Early settlers cherished the food as a staple in their diet, eating them fresh from the bush or in soups, stews and desserts. A pigment called anthrocynin produces the bold blue color of the blueberry. One of the easiest foods to prepare and serve, blueberries need no peeling, pitting or cutting and can easily be frozen (unwashed) for later use. North America is the world's leader in blueberry production.

Cherries Sweet (Prunus avium) and Tart (Prunus cerasus)

What is the difference between sweet cherries and tart cherries? Sweet cherries are grown primarily for fresh eating. The tart cherry, also called the sour cherry, is widely used for canning and processing to make jams, preserves and pies. Tart cherry pie filling is the number one pie filling sold in the United States. Tart cherries have a distinctive bright red color. While sweet cherries are grown in several parts of the country, tarts are grown primarily in northwestern Michigan and parts of Wisconsin, especially Door County. Door County is one of the oldest fruit-growing areas in North America. The sandy soil, as well as the nearby Lake Michigan tempering the Arctic wind in winter and cooling the hot air of summer, provides an excellent growing environment for cherry trees. Tart cherries are very perishable and are therefore seldom sold fresh. They generally are canned or frozen shortly after harvesting. The majority of Michigan's sweet cherry crop is processed. The main product made with sweets is maraschino cherries.

On average, the United States produce more than 650 million pounds of tart and sweet cherries, with Michigan growing about 75 percent of the tart cherry crop. Less than 1 percent of the tart cherry production is used for fresh use. The Wisconsin Red Cherry Growers group is the primary producer of Wisconsin red tart cherries. Cherry Central, a marketing co-op, is considered the largest sweet cheery manufacturer in Michigan. It has one hundred growers who produce about 3 million pounds of dark, sweet cherries primarily for freezing and canning. The Midwest and Northwest are the only areas that produce cherries for the frozen market.

Cranberries (Vaccinium oxycoccus)

An important component of the Midwest foodways, the state of Wisconsin produces more cranberries than any other state in the country and produces more than half of the entire world's supply. Cranberries were called "sassamanesh" by the American

Indians and "crane berry" by the early settlers because the early flower resembled the head, neck and bill of a sand hill crane. Believed to have been on the table at the first Thanksgiving feast, the berry increased in use by settlers, who used the cranberry as a juice and in jellies and jams. "In the 1880s, a New Jersey grower named John 'Peg Leg' Webb discovered the 'cranberry bounce.' Instead of carrying his crop down from the storage loft of his barn, he poured them down the steps. Only the freshest, firmest fruit reached the bottom; rotten or bruised berries remained on the steps. This discovery led to the invention of bounce boards, which helped growers separate rotten berries that didn't bounce from the fresh ones," according to the Visit Wisconsin Rapids website.

More than 250 growers produce cranberries on about eighteen thousand acres of land throughout Wisconsin. Oceanspray®, one of the leaders in the cranberry industry, was formed in 1930 by three cranberry growers and now has more than six hundred growers, many third- and fourth-generation family growers. About 75 percent of the state's total harvest is processed by Oceanspray®. A small percentage (3–5 percent) of the cranberry crop is sold as fresh fruit; the rest is distributed frozen to both national and international markets.

Grapes (Vitis vitaceae)

Better known as American grapes, both wild and cultivated types grow in the area around Lake Michigan. But Michigan is the only lake state to be ranked as a commercial grower for jams and jellies; most recently, it is thought that the state is on the upswing for wines, too. *V. labrusca* is the predominant grape, with some hybrids grown as well.

Pawpaw (Asimina tribola)

The American traditional folk tune "Way Down Yonder in the Paw Paw Patch" has us "pickin' up pawpaws, and puttin' 'em in our pockets." However, one would need very large pockets, as the pawpaw is the largest edible fruit native to the United States and can weigh from a half to a full pound. It was said that chilled pawpaws were a favorite dessert of George Washington and Thomas Jefferson. Found most commonly near riverbanks, the fruit was the primary source of diet during the last days of the Lewis and Clark expedition. Sometimes referred to as the American custard apple or poor man's banana, the pawpaw is highly nutritious—three times as much vitamin C as an apple and high in magnesium, iron and all the essential amino acids. The pawpaw fruit has a creamy, custard-like flesh and tropical flavor, often described as a combination of mango, pineapple and banana. Sold mainly in rural farmers' markets, the pulp from the flesh can be eaten fresh or cooked, and local delicacies include ice cream, compote, jam, pie, cookies, muffins, custard, beer, wine and smoothie drinks.

Being the official native fruit of Ohio, the state holds an annual Pawpaw Festival in September at the peak of the pawpaw season. Festival attendees can enjoy pawpaw foods, pawpaw beer, pawpaw art and much more. All epicureans are encouraged to enter a favorite pawpaw recipe into the yearly competition.

Peach (Prunus persica): Red Haven

The first peach tree in western Michigan was probably planted by William Burnett, who established a trading post on the west bank of the St. Joseph River a mile upstream from Lake Michigan in the 1780s. Burnett planted an orchard near his post and was credited with having taken great pains in caring for it. When the first permanent settlers reached the area in the late 1820s, they found Burnett's orchard healthy and still bearing fruit. Red Haven is a quality standard for other domestic yellow peaches.

Persimmon (Diospyros virginiana)

The word "persimmon" is a phonetic rendering of "putchamin," used by the American Indians of the Algonquin tribe. Persimmons were traditionally used by Native Americans either freshly fallen from the trees or dried to be eaten later in winter. Early settlers used them in puddings, breads and preserves. Native persimmons ripen in the fall, and the pulp must be strained because of all the seeds in the fruit. Ripe persimmons have a mild flavor similar to sweetened pumpkin, and most recipes call for persimmon pulp. A traditional Midwest holiday treat would include persimmon pudding, a baked pudding with the consistency of custard, best eaten warm with whipped cream or vanilla ice cream.

> *Aunt Cleo's Persimmon Pudding*
> *(circa 1930)*
>
> *1 stick (¼ pound) butter melted*
> *2 cups persimmon pulp*
> *1½ cups sugar*
> *1½ cups milk (regular milk or canned)*
> *3 eggs*
> *2 cups flour*
> *1 medium sweet potato, grated*
> *1 teaspoon baking soda*
> *1 teaspoon allspice*
> *1 teaspoon cloves*
> *1 cup coconut (optional)*
>
> *Combine. Bake in 300° F oven for one hour or until done. A broiler pan is a nice size to bake it in.*

Plum (Prunus americana)

Indigenous to the Lake Michigan states region, Native Americans used various parts of the plants. Contemporary uses are predominantly for canned products, jams and or jellies.

Pumpkin (Cucurbita moschata)

The Oxford English Dictionary notes that "a recipe from pumpkin was among the first cookery recipes to have originated in what is today the United States." Illinois and

Indiana are two of the top five pumpkin producing states. According to the Illinois Department of Agriculture, 95 percent of the U.S. crop intended for processing is grown in Illinois.

Rhubarb (Rheum rhapponticum)

Rhubarb is also called the "pie plant" of the United States. Author Lydia Child, of the *American Frugal Housewife* (1833, twelfth edition), wrote, "Rhubarb stalks, or the Persian Apples is the earliest ingredients for pies, which the spring offers." Michigan is one of the top three growers in the United States.

Strawberries (Fragaria spp)

Indigenous to North America, this fruit was discovered in 1588 by Europeans. Native Americans did not cultivate it until there was a demand from the European settlers.

SWEETENERS

Sweetening ingredients are plentiful and important in bake shops. They are food for yeast, are used as a creaming agent when prepared with fats and eggs, give color, create texture and stability when cooked to different temperatures and create tenderness by weakening the gluten structure—not to mention the most obvious, sweetening the product. Syrup sweeteners will provide extra moisture to baked goods.

The word "sugar" is applied to a number of carbohydrate sweeteners. For most bake shops and home bakers, sugar derives from sugar cane (*Saccharum*), a perennial tall grass, or sugar beets (*Beta vulgaris*), a domesticated beet plant. About 35 percent of sugar originates from beets and 65 percent from sugar cane. Technology processes the products so perfectly that they are identical in end product. Sucrose, the chemical name for sugar, is a disaccharide made up of fructose (fruit sugar) bonded with dextrose (glucose). Sucrose is the barometer of sweetness.

Sugar, Sucrose and Sugar Refined Products

The sugar industry has no standard system of labeling sugar grain size. Therefore, manufacturers use different names for varying sizes.

Granulated sugar, table sugar (or sometimes, fine granulated), is the most common.

Sanding sugars have larger grains and are used for coating and decorating products.

Very fine sugar (caster sugar) is finer than granulated sugar. Cake and cookie batters tend to be smooth, absorbing greater amounts of fat and allowing for greater incorporation of air.

Powdered sugar/confectioners' sugar/icing sugar are ground into a fine powder with cornstarch (3 percent) to prevent lumps. They are classified by fineness and coarseness. 10X is the finest sugar, and it is excellent for icings. 6X is the one most available for home bakers, being also used for icings and fillings. Coarser types, like 4X and 2X, are used for dusting.

Molasses, also labeled a syrup, is brown in color and is a byproduct of the sugar refining process. *Sulfured molasses*, in particular, is the purest form and is distinct with mineral flavors. *Blackstrap molasses* is the darkest and is hardly used in contemporary human food production. *Unsulfured molasses* is not a sugar byproduct but rather a manufactured product. The taste is less bitter.

Brown sugar contains varying amounts of molasses, added back into it after it is refined. A soft sugar texture occurs due to this molasses addition. Commercially, it is available in several grades and is given a number to tell how dark it is. The highest number indicates the darkest sugar.

Turbinado sugar is a brown sugar in which some of the molasses is left in during the process of being refined. The molasses in this sugar yields hard crystal results.

Inverted Sugars

Inverted sugars are 30 percent sweeter than sucrose. When sucrose is heated with an acid, it breaks into equal parts of dextrose and levulose. Moisture and resistance to crystallization are attributes of inverted sugars. Bees provide us with a natural inverted sugar in honey. Yet honey is also considered a syrup. This product provides moisture, as well as a fantastically sweet, healthy and natural product. Commercially produced inverted sugars are also available. Easy to blend into various ingredients, syrups are readily available. Moisture is also an added feature that this product brings to sweet baked goods.

Honey is available in syrup form; it is a naturally occurring inverted sugar. Honey has seen a resurgence in recipe production due to its natural health benefits.

Glucose syrup is the legal name for nutritive sweeteners made by the hydrolysis of starch. Literally meaning "reaction with water," hydrolysis is a chemical process in which a molecule is cleaved into two parts by the addition of a molecule of water. The name of where the starch originates may replace the word "glucose" in the name of the syrup. Corn syrup is a prevalent example in sweet baking. If a recipe calls for glucose syrup, corn syrup may be substituted. In the United States, corn syrup is prevalent, whereas in Europe syrups may be prepared from wheat or potato starch.

Corn syrup, beginning as a cornstarch, is converted by the use of enzymes. A liquid sweetener, cornstarch is composed of dextrin (vegetable gum), water, dextrose (also called glucose) and various sugars. Corn syrup is not as sweet as granulated sugar, but it adds moisture to baked goods.

Malt syrup, also called malt extract, is more prevalent in sweet yeast breads rather than in cakes and pastries. Extracted from barley, the malt adds flavor and color and "feeds" the yeast to ferment more rapidly.

Maple syrup is made by concentrating the sap from the sugar maple tree. The sap is boiled, evaporating some water to the syrup consistency desired. The syrup will vary in flavor due to climate, time of season for harvest and soil. Maple syrup is graded by color—light is considered to be the best, amber is second and dark is used mostly for baking and cooking. Modern bakeries rarely use maple syrup, but confectioners and traditional recipes may still call for this ingredient.

Syrups

Honey has continued to be used in baking, but not necessarily in commercial production. Honey baked products are expensive, and some consumers may not be interested in purchasing them. Ironically, natural, organic, local and sustainable products have given new purpose to honey. Honey is a natural sweetener and is considered to be healthier than sugar. It is also considered better for one's health to consume honey made from local bees. Consumers are also requesting products made with local ingredients. Local honey is beginning to be available in local baked goods. Honey is everywhere!

Corn syrup/glucose syrup are not quite identical but are used interchangeably in baking; they have become a desirable choice for home and professional sweet bakers. Not to be confused with high fructose corn syrup, which is used primarily in the soft drink industry.

High fructose corn syrup is corn syrup that has undergone the process to convert the glucose into fructose and then mixed with pure corn syrup (100 percent glucose). This controversial sweetener now has hard evidence that consuming it in excessive quantities leads to "obesity, weight gain, abdominal fat, and a rise in circulating blood fats called triglycerides…Even when rats are fed a high-fat diet, you don't see this; they don't all gain extra weight," according to Hilary Parker's "A Sweet Problem." Not just a soft drink sweetener anymore, corn syrup is used in many commercial sweet baked goods.

Flavorings

Many food products contribute flavors in sweet baking. Flavoring is essentially an extract added to a food or drink to give it a certain taste. Flavorings can also be categorized as natural and artificial. Select what is best for your baking needs.

Cocoa is the dry product left after the cocoa butter is removed from the chocolate liquor, all deriving from the cocoa bean. *Dutch processed cocoa powder* has a higher alkaline. The name is derived from a Dutch inventor who invented a darker and "richer" flavored product. This name has stayed with the product for more than one hundred years.

Chocolate is a recipe! Not all chocolate is created equal, but all are derived from a cocoa bean that has been roasted to give a selected flavor profile (similar to roasting coffee beans). Each chocolate producer decides on the ratio of milk products, sugar, cocoa butter and chocolate liquor (no alcohol, just an industry name for the liquid), as well as any other additional ingredients that may be added.

Unsweetened or *Bitter Chocolate* has no sugar; straight chocolate liquor is referred to as bitter and is bitter in taste.

Sweet Chocolate is bitter chocolate with the cocoa butter and sugar added. Industry standards regulate labeling amounts of cocoa liquor to be able to call it "sweet." *Couverture* chocolate (French for "coating") is usually used to cover and coat cookies, cakes and candies, giving it a wonderful quality flavor. (Do not confuse coating chocolate with couverture, as some coatings have additional fats added for easy melting.)

Milk Chocolate is the sweet chocolate that has milk solids added to it. This product has low cocoa liquor.

White Chocolate is cocoa butter plus sugar and milk solids but without cocoa solids, giving this product its white appearance.

Salt is more than just a seasoning in baking; it also functions to inhibit yeast growth and strengthen gluten structure, allowing for a strong, durable bread texture. Salt must be an exact measurement, as too much could slow fermentation. On the other hand, too little salt rapidly increase fermentation.

Kosher or *table salt* may be used in baking interchangeably. If a recipe has a short baking time, as in delicate cookie baking, be sure that your batter/dough sits long enough to absorb the larger, coarse kosher salt.

Sea salt, naturally without any iodine, is quite different from "table salt" in flavor profile. Some of these salts are colored from the ocean's mineral content, as in black sea salt from Hawaiian water from volcanic ash. Some sea salts are used for the top application in baking (sea salt brownies). The salt is sprinkled on top.

Spices are dried plant or vegetables used to flavor foods. Plant parts may include seeds, roots and bark. Spices have a greater aroma and flavor when freshly ground. Common spices in a professional sweet bake shop may include allspice, anise, caraway, cardamom, cinnamon, cloves, ginger, mace, nutmeg, poppy seeds and sesame seeds. Not necessarily spices, the outer skins of the following citrus fruits (the zests) also add flavor: lemon, orange, lime and grapefruit.

Vanilla is the only edible orchid flower and it is a valuable flavoring agent. Vanilla comes in various forms depending on its use in the bake shop. It is cultivated in various countries around the world: Mexico, Madagascar, French Polynesia and Central and South America.

Vanilla beans are sold individually or packed in quantities by distributors. This ripened, partially dried flower can be sliced open to reveal vanilla seeds. The seeds are scraped into sauces, custards and batters. Vanilla seeds exemplify quality (and a "real" use of the vanilla product).

Vanilla paste has a syrup-like consistency, with vanilla seeds and strong flavor.

Vanilla extract is created when vanilla beans are soaked in an alcohol solution, absorbing the desired strength of flavor. Pure and imitation vanilla extract contain 35 percent alcohol.

Vanilla powder is a newer market product; this powder form can be used for liquid-sensitive products and for toppings.

Extracts are flavorful oils and other ingredients dissolved in alcohol, such as almond, peppermint, spearmint, lemon, cinnamon, coffee, mocha and so on.

CONTEMPORARY SWEET BAKING RECIPES

In many ways, this recipe section was an area I thought about early in my material. It was difficult to select a specific number of recipes. I could have filled this section with so many more! The recipes are a compilation from years of baking—with family, at our gourmet deli, restaurants, family recipes, bakeries, hotels, schools, churches, soup kitchens, trials and errors and customer favorites. It is, without a doubt, just a brief selection reflecting a sweet baker's middle state collection, but certainly it's a mix from differing immigrant groups from Wisconsin, Indiana, Michigan and Illinois.

A traditional gas oven is used for these recipes. If you use a convection oven, keep in mind that the temperature should be lowered on your oven by 25–50 degrees and your baking time is *usually* cut in half. Also, a dark-lined pan increases the likelihood of browning and speeds up baking, too. Lower your oven temperature by 25 degrees in order not to brown the exterior of the product before it is internally done baking. I do not recommend using the convection oven for yeast products. Often the center is not fully baked when the exterior is browned.

QUICK BREADS

As the category suggests, these recipes are "quick" to prepare and should not be overmixed. This can produce a tough final product. Remember, this dough can be placed into varying shapes: muffin, mini-loaf, large loaf and decorator pans. Note: If you are baking your product and notice the top browning quickly, yet your batter is still wet in the center, cover it with foil so your product does not burn.

Pumpkin Gingerbread Muffins

Yield: 1 dozen muffins

1 ½ cups sugar
½ cup oil
2 eggs
1 ¾ cups all-purpose flour
1 teaspoon baking soda
1 teaspoon salt
¼ teaspoon baking powder
1 teaspoon ginger
½ teaspoon each, cinnamon, nutmeg, cloves and allspice
⅓ cup water
8 ounces pumpkin puree

Preheat oven 350 degrees. Spray or line muffin tins with muffin papers. Mix sugar, oil and eggs. Sift flour, soda, powder and salt. Mix remaining spices and flavorings to the flour mixture. Whisk in wet sugar, oil and egg mixture, alternating pumpkin and water. Fill muffin cups ⅔ to top. Bake 15–20 minutes or until toothpick comes out clean and/or when product "springs back" when touched.

Chocolate Cinnamon Loaf

Yield: 1 loaf

1 cup sugar
½ cup (1 stick) unsalted butter, room temperature
2 cups all-purpose flour
1 teaspoon baking powder
1 teaspoon baking soda
8 ounces sour cream
1 teaspoon vanilla extract
2 large eggs
2 ounces of semisweet chocolate
1 teaspoon cinnamon

Preheat oven to 350 degrees. Butter and flour 9 x 5-inch loaf pan. Beat sugar and butter in a large bowl until light and fluffy. Stir flour, baking powder and baking soda into butter mixture. Beat just until blended. Add sour cream and vanilla and beat just until smooth. Beat in eggs.

Spread half of batter into prepared pan. Sprinkle chocolate with cinnamon over batter. Spread remaining batter over chocolate mixture. Sprinkle top with remaining chocolate mixture. Using knife, swirl chocolate mixture into batter. Bake loaf until tester in center comes out clean, about 55 minutes. Cool 10 minutes and remove loaf from pan.

Honey Raisin Bran Muffins

Yield: 1½ dozen muffins

½ cup unsalted butter
½ cup honey
2 eggs
2½ cups all-purpose flour
2½ cups bran
4 teaspoons baking powder
½ teaspoon salt
2 cups milk
2 cups raisins

Preheat oven 350 degrees. Cream butter and honey; add eggs one at a time until incorporated. Mix dry ingredients alternately with milk into the wet ingredients. Mix in raisins. Spray or line muffin tins with muffin papers. Bake 15–20 minutes or until toothpick comes out clean and/or when product "springs back" when touched.

Peanut Butter–Chocolate Chip Muffins

Yield: 1½ dozen muffins

1¾ cups all-purpose flour
1 cup sugar
1 tablespoon baking powder
¾ cup milk
¾ cup peanut butter (smooth or chunky)
⅓ cup oil
1 egg
½ cup chocolate chips

Preheat oven 350 degrees. Blend oil, sugar, peanut butter and egg. Add alternately with milk to flour and baking powder. Mix just until blended; fold in chocolate chips. Bake 15–20 minutes or until toothpick comes out clean and/or when product "springs back" when touched.

Carrot Tea Bread
Yield: 4 mini-loafs

3 eggs
1 cup oil
2 cups sugar
1 tablespoon vanilla extract
3 cups flour
2 cups peeled and shredded carrots
½ teaspoon salt
½ teaspoon baking soda
1 teaspoon cinnamon

Preheat oven 350 degrees. Whisk eggs, oil, sugar and vanilla in bowl. Stir in carrots. Mix in remaining ingredients until well blended. Bake 15–20 minutes or until toothpick comes out clean and/or when product "springs back" when touched.

Apricot Bran and Flax Muffins
Yield: 1½ dozen

1½ cups oat bran
1 cup brown sugar
1 cup all-purpose flour
1 cup buttermilk
1 cup flaxseed (may be ground)
½ cup canola oil
1 cup bran
2 eggs
1 tablespoon baking powder
1 teaspoon baking soda
½ teaspoon salt
1½ cups raisins
2 cups peeled and skinned or canned and drained apricots

In a large bowl, combine oat bran, flour, flaxseed, bran, baking powder and salt. Set aside. In a food processor, combine apricots, brown sugar, buttermilk, oil, eggs and baking soda. Blend well. Pour apricot mixture into dry ingredients. Mix. Stir in raisins. Fill muffin tins. Bake in a preheated 375° F oven for 18–20 minutes or until toothpick comes out clean.

FRIED DOUGHS

Doughs or batters for doughnuts, churros and crullers will either have yeast or baking powder or soda for leavening. But all are fried in fat: oil, lard or shortening. Your fat will certainly have an impact on the final flavor. Warm and fresh are the keys to these recipes.

Buttermilk Spice Doughnuts
Yield: about 1 dozen

3½ cups flour
¼ cup unsalted butter, melted
2 teaspoons baking powder
2 eggs, beaten
½ teaspoon salt
¼ teaspoon baking soda
1 teaspoon allspice
⅔ cup buttermilk
⅔ cup sugar

Sift together flour, baking powder, salt and allspice. Set aside. In a large mixing bowl, blend melted butter and sugar. Beat in eggs until mixture is smooth. Stir baking soda into buttermilk and beat until foamy.

Add to sugar and egg mixture. Stir in dry ingredients. Batter will be stiff. Add extra flour if necessary. Chill dough until firm and cool (30 minutes). Roll out on a floured surface to ½-inch thickness. Cut circles or squares in desired size. Let stand 20 minutes before frying in hot fat or oil, 375 degrees. Drain on paper towel and roll in cinnamon sugar mixture (1 cup sugar, 2 teaspoons cinnamon).

Churros (Mexican-style fried dough)

Yield: 6 servings

1 cup all-purpose flour
4 large eggs
2 teaspoons sugar
½ teaspoon salt
¼ cup (½ stick) unsalted butter
1 cup whole milk
3 cups oil (canola preferred) for frying

In saucepan, bring milk, butter, sugar and salt to a boil, stirring until dissolved. Remove pot from heat and stir in flour. Place back over the heat, stirring constantly. Cook until dough is shiny, about 2 minutes. Transfer immediately to an electric mixer bowl. Using paddle attachment and add eggs one at a time.

Pipe immediately from a pastry bag using a star tip or plain tip, 4–6 in. each in length. Heat oil to 350 degrees; cook dough until lightly browned, about 2 minutes per side.

Toss in cinnamon sugar mixture (1 cup sugar and 2 teaspoons cinnamon).

Crullers
(early nineteenth-century Dutch "kruller" means "to curl")
Yield: 2 dozen

4 cups sifted all-purpose flour
¼ pound butter
1 ½ cups confectioners' sugar
3 eggs, well beaten
½ teaspoon cinnamon
¼ teaspoon nutmeg
3 cups oil or shortening for frying

In a large bowl, combine flour, sugar, cinnamon and nutmeg. With a fork or pastry blender, blend the butter in the flour mixture until all fat is coated. Stir in eggs to form a dough, adding a little water as necessary. Knead dough well on floured board. (This dough can be made in an electric mixer using dough hook; knead about 4 minutes until dough is shiny and adheres to hook.)

Roll dough into squares ½-inch thick. Cut into narrow ½-inch strips. Twist strips into various shapes. Fry at 400 degrees until golden. Sprinkle with confectioners' sugar.

Amish Doughnuts

1 package dry yeast in ¼ cup warm water
1 tablespoon sugar or honey
¾ cup sugar
¾ cup lard
2 egg yolks
1 tablespoon salt
3 cups flour

Cream ingredients together. Then add yeast mixture. Beat again. Add 4 cups lukewarm water. Add 3 cups flour to a make a soft dough. Let stand 1 ½ hours in refrigerator. Take amount you need out. Roll out into desired size. Raise another 1 hour. Fry in deep fat, 350 degrees. Glaze or roll in powdered sugar.

CRUMBLES AND CRISPS

Most Midwest fruits—canned, frozen or fresh—may be substituted or combined for these recipes. Seasonal fruit is always delightful!

Cherry Crumble

Yield: 6 servings

1 pound fresh cherries (pitted or frozen cherries, thawed and drained)
½ cup plus 1 tablespoon sugar
1 teaspoon cornstarch
4 large eggs
¼ cup almonds, toasted
⅓ cup all-purpose flour
pinch of salt
1 cup whole milk
¼ cup unsalted butter, melted
1 teaspoon grated lemon peel
1 teaspoon vanilla extract
(½ teaspoon almond extract—optional)

Preheat oven to 325 degrees. Butter shallow dish (1½ quart baking dish). Combine cherries, 1 tablespoon sugar and cornstarch in bowl; toss to coat. Place cherries in bottom of dish.

Topping: Blend flour and almonds in food processor until nuts are finely chopped. Whisk eggs, salt and remaining ½ cup sugar in large bowl to blend. Whisk in flour mixture. Add milk, butter, lemon peel and vanilla and almond extracts; whisk until smooth. Pour over mixture over cherries.

Peach Crisp with a Cornmeal Cinnamon Streusel

Yield: 6 servings

6 cups peeled and sliced peaches
1 teaspoon lemon juice
3 tablespoons sugar
pinch of salt

STREUSEL
½ cup brown sugar
1 teaspoon ground cinnamon
½ cup all-purpose flour
½ cup yellow cornmeal
4 ounces (1 stick) cold unsalted butter

Preheat oven to 350 degrees. Generously butter a 2-quart oven-proof dish. Combine sliced peaches with sugar, lemon juice and salt; coat thoroughly.

Streusel: Put all streusel ingredients in a food processor and pulse until mixture is pea-sized. If preparing by hand, combine dry ingredients and use pastry blender or fork and mash butter into the dry mixture until pea-sized. Sprinkle streusel over the peaches. Bake for 30 minutes until streusel is lightly browned and mixture bubbles. Serve warm.

Blueberry Cobbler

Yield: 8 servings

6 cups blueberries
2 tablespoons tapioca flour
5 tablespoons sugar
1 teaspoon freshly squeezed lemon juice
pinch salt

COBBLER TOPPING
2 cups flour
½ teaspoon salt
¼ cup brown sugar, firmly packed
2 teaspoons baking powder
¾ stick unsalted butter
¾ cup heavy cream whipping cream

Preheat oven to 350 degrees. Gently combine the blueberries with the tapioca flour, sugar, lemon juice and salt in a large bowl. Place mixture in a buttered oven-proof dish.

Topping: Combine all dry ingredients in a bowl. Add butter with pastry blender or by using the paddle attachment on a mixer. Mix and add cream slowly. Mix just until combined. On a lightly floured board, roll the dough until ½-in. thick. Cut into pieces about 1 inch or in shapes (stars if you have a star cookie cutter). Place on top of the berry mixture. Brush a little extra cream on top of the dough and sprinkle with sugar (optional).

Bake for 25–30 minutes until crust is golden brown or mixture is bubbling. Serve with whip cream.

COOKIES

Bagged, rolled, dropped, molded, icebox, sheet, bar and stencil all are ways to form cookies. Because cookies' baking time is usually short, having uniform-sized cookies is important, especially if they are on the same baking tray.

Sparkling Sour Cream Sugar Cookies
Yield: 3 dozen

¾ cup butter, softened
1 cup granulated sugar
1 teaspoon baking powder
¼ teaspoon baking soda
dash of salt
½ cup sour cream
1 egg
1 teaspoon shredded orange peel (zest)
½ teaspoon lemon extract
2½ cups all-purpose flour

In mixing bowl, beat butter with electric mixer 30 seconds. Add sugar, baking powder, soda and salt; beat well. Beat in sour cream, egg, peel and lemon extract. Beat in as much flour as you can with the mixer. Using a wooden spoon, stir in remaining flour. Divide in half. Cover chill until firm. On a well-floured surface, roll out half of the dough at a time to ¼-inch thickness. Using a cookie cutter, cut dough into desired shapes. Place cookies 1 inch apart on an ungreased cookie sheet. Bake in a 375° F oven for 6–7 minutes or until edges are firm and bottoms are light brown.

Magic Cookie Bars
Yield: 2 dozen bars

½ cup butter
1 (8 ounces) package semisweet chocolate chips
1½ cups graham cracker crumbs
3½ ounces shredded coconut
1 (14 ounces) sweetened condensed milk
1 cup chopped walnuts

Preheat oven to 350° F. In a 9 x 13-in. baking pan, melt butter and sprinkle crumbs over butter. Pour sweetened condensed milk evenly over crumbs. Top evenly with chocolate chips, coconut and nuts. Press down gently. Bake 25–30 minutes or until lightly browned. Cool thoroughly before cutting.

Three-Ginger Cookies
Yield: 2½ dozen

¾ cup unsalted butter, softened
1 cup dark brown sugar
¼ cup molasses
1 egg
2¼ cups flour
2 teaspoons ground ginger
2 teaspoons baking soda
½ teaspoon salt
1½ tablespoons chopped ginger
½ cup chopped crystallized ginger

Cream butter and brown sugar. Beat in molasses and egg. Sift flour, ground ginger, baking soda and salt together and add to butter mixture. Stir with a wooden to blend. Add the other gingers and mix well. Refrigerate dough for at least 2 hours. Grease a cookie sheet or cover with parchment. Roll dough into 1-in. ball and roll tops of balls in granulated sugar. Bake at 350 degrees for 8–10 minutes, until brown around edges.

Chocolate-Nut Biscotti

Yield: 3 dozen

⅔ cup whole almonds or pistachios (3 ounces)
pinch of salt
¾ cup plus 2 tablespoons all-purpose flour
2 large eggs, at room temperature
3½ ounces milk chocolate, chopped
1 teaspoon pure vanilla extract
½ cup sugar
1 large egg white, beaten
¼ cup plus 2 tablespoons unsweetened cocoa powder
1 pound semisweet tempered chocolate (optional)

Preheat oven to 300 degrees. Spread the nuts in pie plate and toast them in the oven until golden brown, about 20 minutes. Transfer the nuts to a plate and let them cool completely. Raise temperature to 350 degrees. In a food processor, combine the flour with milk chocolate and process until the mixture resembles coarse meal. Add the sugar, cocoa powder and salt and pulse to mix. Add the beaten whole eggs and the vanilla and process until dough forms. Transfer the dough to a lightly floured surface and knead in the toasted nuts. Divide the dough in half. On a lightly floured work surface, roll each piece of dough into a foot-long log. Transfer the logs to a baking sheet lined with parchment paper or foil and flatten them slightly. Lightly brush the logs with the beaten egg white and bake for about 30 minutes, or until firm to the touch and slightly cracked. Remove from the oven and let cool for 1 minute. Turn the oven down to 325 degrees. Transfer hot logs to a work surface, and using a serrated knife, slice the logs ⅓- to ½-inch thick.

Arrange the biscotti standing (on their sides) but separated from one another and bake for another 5 minutes. Completely cool. If dipping biscotti, melt tempered chocolate, dip into mixture and let cool on lined parchment tray.

Butterscotch Icebox Cookies

Yield: 2 dozen

8 ounces butter
8 ounces brown sugar
1 teaspoon salt
3 eggs
2 teaspoons vanilla extract
¼ teaspoon baking soda
12 ounces pastry flour

Cream butter and sugar, adding eggs one at a time until fully incorporated. Add vanilla extract to butter mixture. Sift dry ingredients together (salt, soda and flour) and add in batches to the butter mixture. Take a 12 × 12-in. piece of wax paper, parchment or plastic wrap and lay flat on counter. Take cookie dough and place on lower half of parchment. Spread dough mixture across paper in long tube shape. Using the parchment, roll the dough while shaping to the thickness you desire for your cookie. A large roll will give you big cookies. Wrap parchment around cookie dough firmly. Twist or tie ends of parchment. Refrigerate until chilled, about 1 hour. Preheat oven to 350 degrees. Unwrap cookie dough; slice and bake until slightly brown or somewhat firm on the edges, 8–10 minutes.

Black Walnut Bars

Yield: 1 dozen 1½-inch bar cookies

1½ cups black walnuts, chopped
1½ cups graham cracker crumbs
1 14-ounce can of sweetened condensed milk
pinch of salt

Preheat oven to 325 degrees. Put graham cracker crumbs and black walnuts into a medium-sized bowl. Slowly add condensed milk and salt. Mix thoroughly. Press and pack into a nonstick 8-inch-square pan. If you do not have nonstick, line with parchment paper. Take a rubber spatula or off-set spatula (sprayed with nonstick vegetable spray) and smooth top of mixture. Bake for 25–30 minutes. Cool and cut.

Elephant Ears (miniature)

Yield: 2 dozen

1 sheet, thawed, puff pastry sheet
1 cup granulated sugar
½ cup unsalted melted butter

Sprinkle sugar on the table, in place of flour, and roll puff pastry until ⅛-in. thick and as long as desired. (A shorter width of dough will yield a larger cookie when rolled.) As you roll the pastry, try to keep the dough in a rectangular shape. Brush with melted butter and sprinkle with desired amount of sugar. Identify the center of the dough and roll dough from either side up into a spiral or scroll. Each scroll should be the same thickness. Freeze until slightly firm. Slice ½-in. thick. Refreeze until slices are frozen and place on ungreased oven tray. Bake in a preheated oven at 425 degrees. Bake until lightly brown, 8–12 minutes.

Peanut Butter Sandwich Cookies

Yield: 2 dozen

½ cup whole wheat pastry flour
¾ cup all-purpose flour
½ cup confectioners' sugar
3 tablespoons cocoa powder
¼ teaspoon baking powder
½ cup unsalted and chilled butter, cubed
1 teaspoon vanilla extract
1 medium egg
2 ounces semi/bittersweet chocolate, grated

Preheat oven to 400 degrees. Combine all dry ingredients into a bowl. Cut in cold butter, until pea sized, using a pastry blender or electric mixer (paddle attachment). In a separate bowl, combine egg, vanilla and grated chocolate. Add to flour/butter mixture until stiff dough forms. Between two pieces of parchment (or plastic wrap), roll the batter, using no flour. Roll until ⅜-in. thickness and chill for 30 minutes. Cut into desired shapes, placed apart on sheet pan. Chill again for another 20 minutes. Bake for 4–6 minutes, until cookie surface is slightly dry.

<u>PEANUT BUTTER FILLING</u>
½ cup unsalted butter
I cup confectioners' sugar
⅓ cup creamy peanut butter

Soften butter and add sugar using pastry blender or electric mixer; add peanut butter and thoroughly combine. Use a piping bag or spoon, place filling between two cookies and enjoy.

Linzer Cookies
Yield: 3 dozen

3 ounces, toasted and ground almonds
2 cups powdered sugar
2 tablespoons lemon zest, finely grated
½ teaspoon almond extract
3½ cups all-purpose flour, sifted
½ teaspoon salt
13 ounces unsalted butter (3 sticks plus 2 tablespoons), softened
I egg, whisked
2 cups raspberry jam (with or without seeds)
(½ teaspoon cinnamon—optional)

Cream the butter and sugar in an electric mixer until light and fluffy. Add egg, zest and extract. Combine flour and salt in small batches until combined. Add nuts until blended. Divide the dough into two pieces. Wrap and refrigerate until well chilled. Preheat oven to 350 degrees. Remove two portions of dough from the refrigerator. When soft enough to roll, 5–10 minutes, roll to ⅛-in. Using a 2-inch cookie cutter, cut cookies. Transfer cookie bottoms to one sheet pan; taking a small cookie cutter, cut out the center of the other half of the cookies. The cookies with the cutout centers will be the tops. Bake 10–12 minutes. Cool. Take bottom cookie and spread with raspberry jam, place cutout center top cookie on top.

PIES AND TARTS

What is the difference between a pie and a tart? First and foremost—and really the major difference—is the pan itself. A tart pan has vertical sides that are sharp and traditionally fluted. Thank goodness for a drop-out bottom, as it helps remove the entire tart in perfect form. Pie pans have sloped edges and tend to be deeper than a tart pan. Fillings for both are limitless and up to your imagination. Sometimes a tart has pastry cream with fruits on top, but at other times it can have a basic poured cream filling with baked fruits, too. Pies for this section are sweet, but of course they can be savory as well. Custards, creams and chiffon pies are sometimes cold and poured into a prebaked pie crust, with a stabilizer (gelatin and cornstarch) added to help them "set." The American-style cookies and crusts are also fun and delicious.

Shoo-Fly Pie

CRUST
1½ cups pastry flour
½ cup lard
¼ cup water
1 teaspoon salt

Place measured flour and salt in a bowl or on table. Make a well, or center, in the middle of the flour and salt mixture. Take a fork or pastry cutter and blend in the lard; it will look lumpy. Add water, just until mixed. Do not overmix, as the pastry will become tough. Chill until firm. Spray pie pan with nonstick shortening. Flour working surface and roll dough into a circular shape to fit the pan. Roll to ½-in. thickness, allowing dough to overhang pie plate at first. Press dough into pan and up onto the sides. Remove any air bubbles. Crimp edges of dough by hand or with fork tines. Chill until cool. Preheat oven to 400 F.

SYRUP
½ cup molasses
½ cup maple syrup
¼ cup dark corn syrup
1 teaspoon baking soda
2 eggs, beaten
¾ cup boiling water
¼ teaspoon cloves
¼ teaspoon cinnamon

Dissolve baking soda in boiling water. Stir in both syrups and molasses with cloves and cinnamon. Blend all liquids. When cool, whisk in eggs and pour into the unbaked crust.

TOPPING
1 cup flour
½ cup brown sugar
¼ cup lard or butter
¼ teaspoon nutmeg
½ teaspoon cinnamon

Cream butter/lard with sugar and spices. Add flour but leave in pea-sized pieces. Sprinkle on top of pie. Bake for 10 minutes at 400 degrees and then reduce to 350 degrees for 50 minutes.

Apple Tart with Salted Caramel Butter

SWEET PASTRY
1¼ cups butter
1 cup sugar
2 eggs
3½ cups all-purpose flour
1 teaspoon vanilla

Using a mixer with paddle attachment (or by hand with a pastry blender), mix the butter and the sugar, adding the eggs one at a time. Add vanilla. Chill dough. Roll out to fit one large tart mold or a half-dozen individual tart molds.

Press dough into pan and up onto the sides. Remove any air bubbles. Crimp edges of dough by hand or with fork tines. Chill until cool.

Preheat oven to 400 F. Using tinfoil, line the top of the dough with the foil and use pie weights or uncooked beans to "weigh" down the crust. Bake for about 15 minutes, until edges are set. Remove foil and bake until crust is light brown.

CARAMEL
½ cup sugar
1 tablespoon water
1 cup evaporated milk
⅓ cup salted butter

Select a thick-bottomed sauce or sauté pan. Cook water and sugar until water completely evaporates and sugar begins to brown (carmelize). Carefully add the evaporated milk stirring rapidly; add butter. Set aside.

Fruit Filling
4 red apples cut into cubes (do not remove skins)
⅔ cups dark or golden raisins
2 tablespoons walnuts, chopped
2 tablespoons pistachios
½ cup butter, unsalted

Cook apples on stove top with raisins and butter until soft but still firm. Add nuts toward the end, stirring to coat with butter. Mix in half the caramel. Spread the apples and dried fruit into the tart and pour the remaining caramel across.

Brown Sugar Pecan Pie

Crust
5 ounces unsalted butter
4 ounces light brown sugar
½ of one entire egg after whisking
7 ounces bread flour

Place butter, brown sugar and egg in a mixing bowl. Mix at low speed, using the dough hook attachment, until the ingredients are just combined. Add flour and continue to mix until dough is smooth. Refrigerate until firm. Preheat oven to 350 degrees. Roll out dough to fit the pie pan, flouring counter as necessary. Roll to ¼-inch thick.

Pecan Filling
3 eggs
1 cup sugar
2 tablespoons butter, melted
1 teaspoon vanilla extract
1 cup pecans, chopped
1 cup corn syrup

Whisk all ingredients together and pour into unbaked pie crust. Bake 45–50 minutes until pie is firm.

Espresso-Chocolate Tart

TART SHELL
1 cup all-purpose flour
¾ teaspoon salt
⅓ cup cocoa powder
½ cup (1 stick) unsalted butter, softened
¼ cup sugar
1 large egg
¾ teaspoon vanilla extract
3 tablespoons heavy cream

Sift flour, salt and cocoa powder into a medium bowl; set aside. Cream butter and sugar in electric mixer and add egg and vanilla. Mix until combined. Gradually add flour mixture, alternating with the cream. Shape dough into rectangle, wrap in plastic and refrigerate until cold.

Preheat oven to 350 degrees. Roll out dough, flouring counter as necessary. Roll to ¼-inch thick. Grease circular or rectangle tart pan. Press dough into the pan and prick with fork. Line unbaked dough with parchment and weigh down with uncooked beans or pie weights. Bake until slightly firm, 10 minutes. Remove parchment and weights; continue to bake until brown, 20 minutes total.

GANACHE
1¼ cups heavy cream
2 tablespoons ground espresso beans
8 ounces bittersweet chocolate, chopped

FILLING
1½ cups mascarpone cheese

Bring cream and espresso to a boil; strain over chopped chocolate in a bowl. Whisk mixture until smooth. Let cool to room temperature. Smooth mascarpone cheese over bottom of baked tart shell. Pour or scoop ganache over the cheese. Refrigerate until chilled.

Sweet Potato Bourbon Pie

Follow pie crust for Shoo-Fly Pie (160) or sweet crust from the Apple Tart with Salted Caramel Butter (161).

<u>Filling</u>
¾ cup sugar
15 ounces sweet potatoes, cooked, peeled and mashed
1 can evaporated milk (12 ounces)
½ teaspoon salt
1 teaspoon cinnamon
½ teaspoon ground ginger
¼ teaspoon ground cloves
2 large eggs
(2 ounces bourbon whiskey—optional)

Whisk eggs, stir in sweet potatoes and bourbon. Mix sugar, salt and spices; add to wet mixture. Gradually stir in evaporated milk. Pour into unbaked pie shell. Bake in a preheated 425° F oven for 15 minutes; reduce temperature to 350 degrees for 40–50 minutes or until knife in center comes out clean. Cool.

CAKES

Cakes are the foundation from which amazing things can be built—sheet cakes, round cakes, stacked cakes and rolled cakes and more. As you measure, scale and prepare your ingredients for cake, the mixing methods and ingredients will determine the end result: chiffon, angel, sponge and so on. Not all cake methods will be included here.

Lemon Mint Pound Cake
Yield: 2 loaves

1½ cups cake flour
1½ cups all-purpose flour
1 teaspoon baking powder
¼ teaspoon salt

1 cup buttermilk
2 tablespoons fresh lemon juice
1 teaspoon vanilla extract
2 cups unsalted butter, softened
2 cups sugar
¼ cup lemon zest
2 tablespoons fresh mint, chopped (or 2 teaspoons mint extract)
4 eggs

Preheat oven to 350 degrees. Spray loaf pan with baking spray. Combine all dry ingredients and sift. In a small bowl, combine buttermilk, vanilla extract and lemon juice. Cream butter. Add sugar and eggs one at a time. Add lemon mixture, zest and mint, scraping down sides of bowl. Add flour in batches, just until incorporated. Pour batter into loaf pan. Bake for 40 minutes or until toothpick inserted comes out clean.

Vanilla Bean Cake

7 tablespoons unsalted butter
7 ounces white chocolate, chopped
2 teaspoons vanilla bean paste or 2 vanilla beans, split and scraped
⅓ cup bread flour
5 eggs, separated
⅓ cup sugar
pinch of cream of tartar

Using a 10-in. spring form pan, butter the insides and line the bottom with parchment paper. Over a double boiler, melt the white chocolate and add butter until almost melted. Remove from heat and add vanilla seeds; stir until smooth. Stir in eggs. Sift bread flour over the batter. Stir. Beat egg whites with cream of tartar to soft peaks, gradually adding sugar. Beat until whites are stiff and glossy. Fold part of the whites into the batter. Fold in remaining, trying not to deflate the egg whites. Pour batter into pan. Refrigerate until cool. Preheat oven to 375 degrees. Bake until toothpick inserted comes out clean, about 30 minutes.

Mexican Chocolate Streusel Cake

CAKE
8 ounces all-purpose flour
½ teaspoon baking powder
8 ounces cream cheese, room temperature
8 ounces butter, softened
5 ounces sugar
4 eggs

Combine cream cheese, butter and sugar in mixer with paddle attachment until light and fluffy. Add eggs; combine. Add flour and baking powder. Mix until just combined. Spray and parchment cake pan.

TOPPING
1 egg yolk
½ teaspoon salt
3 ounces butter, room temperature
1 cup all-purpose flour
1 pound chocolate, chopped
(1 tablespoon cinnamon—optional)

Pulse chocolate in food processor until it becomes coarse crumbs. Add yolks, salt, butter and flour. Combine until crumbly. Crumble topping over batter. Bake 350 degrees, 35–40 minutes, until cake pulls apart from the sides. (Fold in some chocolate and cinnamon to batter—optional.)

Cherry Whiskey Cake

½ cup brown sugar
½ cup granulated sugar
1 cup unsalted butter
2 cups all-purpose flour, sifted
pinch of salt
4 eggs
¼ teaspoon nutmeg
1 cup candied cherries, cut up
2 cups currants or raisins
¾ cup mixed citron and candied orange peel

1 grated lemon for zest
5 tablespoons whiskey

Combine sugars and cream with butter until light and fluffy. Add eggs one at a time. Add nutmeg, lemon zest and whiskey. Add flour with salt into batter. Mix thoroughly. Add fruit and fold in. Bake at 350° F for about 2 to 2½ hours. Sprinkle with a little more whiskey when warm.

COFFEECAKES AND STRUDEL

What is there not to like in a sweet yeast coffeecake, enriched with butter, eggs and sugar (or maybe all three)? The dough by itself can be prepared into a variety of products. The fillings and toppings are endless. Strudel, for this text, is the ready-made phyllo (unleavened paper-thin sheets of dough) leaf dough. This pastry can be purchased from the frozen food section; in some shops, they have it fresh in the refrigerator.

Apple Kuchen (from the Red Star Favorites recipe file)
Yield: one 13 x 9-inch coffeecake

½ cup water
¼ cup milk
¾ cup butter
4 eggs
3 cups bread flour
½ teaspoon salt
¼ cup sugar
4½ teaspoon active dry Red Star Yeast®

BREAD MACHINE METHOD
Have liquid ingredients at 80 degrees and all others at room temperature. Place ingredients in pan in the order listed. Select dough/manual cycle. Do not use the delay timer. After 5 minutes of kneading, open lid of bread machine. Scrape sides of bread pan with rubber spatula, moving the soft batter towards the kneading blade to assist mixing. Do not add additional flour.

HAND-HELD MIXER/STANDARD MIXER METHOD
Combine yeast, 1¾ cup flour and other dry batter ingredients. Combine water, milk and butter; heat to 120 to 130 degrees (butter does not need to melt). Combine dry mixture and warmed liquid ingredients in mixing bowl. Add eggs; blend at low speed until

moistened. Beat 3 minutes at medium speed. Gradually stir in remaining flour by hand to make a soft batter. Place dough in lightly oiled bowl and turn to grease top. Cover. Let rise in warm place until double, about 30 minutes.

FOOD PROCESSOR METHOD
Combine yeast, 1¾ cup flour and other dry batter ingredients. Combine water, milk and butter; heat to 120 to 130 degrees (butter does not need to melt). Let cool to room temperature. Have all other ingredients at room temperature. Put dry mixture in processing bowl with steel blade. While motor is running, add butter, eggs and liquid ingredients. Process until mixed. Continue processing, adding remaining flour until a soft batter forms. Place dough in lightly oiled bowl and turn to grease top. Cover. Let rise in warm place until double, about 30 minutes.

When the batter is ready, stir it down. Spread in greased 13 x 9-inch cake pan. Spoon topping over batter. Cover. Let rest for 10 minutes. Bake in preheated 350° F oven for 45–50 minutes, until golden brown. Serve warm with butter sauce.

TOPPING
3 large apples (4 cups), peeled and sliced
½ cup chopped pecans
⅓ cup sugar
¼ cup butter, melted
1 teaspoon cinnamon
1 teaspoon lemon rind, grated

In medium bowl, combine all topping ingredients.

BUTTER SAUCE
1 cup sugar
½ cup butter
½ cup half-and-half
1 teaspoon vanilla

Combine sugar, butter and half-and-half cream. Heat to boiling. Simmer until thickened. Add vanilla.

Recipe note: You can substitute instant (fast-rising) yeast in place of active dry yeast in batter/no-knead recipes. When using instant yeast, expect your batter/dough to rise about 50 percent faster. Adjust your rise times accordingly. For traditional methods, use equal amounts; for bread machines, use ½ teaspoon instant yeast or ¾ teaspoon active dry yeast per cup of flour in your recipe.

Chocolate Cherry Babka

Known in some countries as Baba, this eastern European product is recognized as a rich yeast risen "cake." It can be shaped in a Bundt pan or rectangular coffeecake shape.

DOUGH
½ cup warm milk (105–115° F)
½ cup plus 2 teaspoons sugar
2 teaspoons active dry yeast
1¾ cups all-purpose flour
1 whole large egg
1 large egg yolk
1 teaspoon pure vanilla extract
½ teaspoon salt
5 tablespoons unsalted butter, cut into pieces and softened

FILLING
3 tablespoons unsalted butter, well softened
1 4-ounce bar fine-quality bittersweet chocolate, finely chopped
¼ cup sugar
1 cup dried cherries, chopped

Stir together warm milk and 2 teaspoons sugar in bowl of mixer. Sprinkle yeast over mixture and let sit until foamy, about 5 minutes. (If yeast doesn't foam, discard and start over with new yeast.)

Add half of flour to yeast mixture and beat at medium speed until combined. Add whole eggs, yolk, vanilla, salt and remaining sugar and beat until combined. Reduce speed to low and then mix in remaining flour, about ½ cup at a time. Increase speed to medium and then beat in butter, a few pieces at a time, and continue to beat until dough is shiny and forms strands from paddle to bowl, about 4 minutes. (Dough will be very soft and sticky.)

Scrape dough into a lightly oiled bowl and cover bowl with plastic wrap. Let dough rise in a draft-free place at warm room temperature until doubled in bulk, 1½ to 2 hours.

BABKAS AND FILLING
Preheat oven to 350° F. Line each loaf pan with parchment paper (1 lengthwise and 1 crosswise).

Punch down dough with a lightly oiled rubber spatula and then halve dough. Roll out one piece of dough on a well-floured surface with a lightly floured rolling pin into an 18-

by 10-inch rectangle and arrange with a long side nearest you. Make an egg wash with 1 egg and a little bit of cream.

Sprinkle half of chocolate evenly over buttered dough and then sprinkle with half of sugar (2 tablespoons). Starting with long side farthest from you, roll dough into a snug log, pinching firmly along egg-washed seam to seal. Loosely cover pan with buttered plastic wrap (buttered side down) and let babka rise until dough reaches top of pans, 1 to 2 hours—or let dough rise in pans in a refrigerator, 8 to 12 hours. Bring to room temperature, 3 to 4 hours, before baking. Bake about 40 minutes or until golden brown.

Apple Raisin Kringle

½ cup butter
½ teaspoon salt
1½ tablespoons sugar
2 cups all-purpose flour
1 package dry yeast
¼ warm milk
¼ cup warm water (110–115° F)
1 egg room temperature, separated

FILLING (COMBINE)
2 chopped apples, skinned and de-seeded
¼ cup raisins
¼ cup brown sugar
2 teaspoons flour

Combine sugar, salt, flour and butter into bowl. Cut fat into dry ingredients. Dissolve yeast in warm water. Scald milk. Cool to lukewarm and blend in egg yolk. Stir yeast mixture well and add to egg yolk moisture. Pour yeast mixture into bowl containing remaining ingredients. Blend. Retard (let rise in cold) in refrigerator, until doubled in height.

Divide dough into two parts. Roll dough into a rectangle (about 6- by 18-inch rectangle). Spread with whipped egg white. Spread filling. Fold side over. Fill the long way and pinch edge of dough into a roll. Shape dough into a circle shape. Let rise until doubled. Bake in a preheated 400° F oven, 25 minutes.

Italian Cranberry Strudel Cheesecake
Yield: 12 servings

12 sheets phyllo dough
½ cup unsalted butter, room temperature
½ cup granulated sugar
1 cup mascarpone cheese
4 egg yolks, room temperature
1½ cups ricotta cheese
1½ teaspoons vanilla extract
1 orange zest, grated
1 lemon zest, grated
4 egg whites
3 ounces of cake flour
1 cup dried cranberries, chopped
½ cup almonds, ground

Combine ¼ cup sugar with butter and mascarpone. Beat until light and fluffy. Add yolks one at a time. Stir in ricotta, vanilla, dried cranberries and zests. Whip egg whites until foamy and add remaining sugar until stiff peaks form. Fold reserved cheese into the meringue. Combine flour and ground almonds; combine fillings.

Unwrap phyllo dough and cover with damp cloth so it does not dry out. Cut paper or parchment about size of phyllo sheets. Brush each layer with melted butter. Continue layering until there is a stack of four. Place one-third of filling horizontally. Fill about 1½ inches from end. Fold in ends of phyllo about ½ inch and roll dough away from you, using paper to help. Seal with melted butter. Chill. Bake in a 375° F oven until golden brown.

ORIGINS AND HISTORIES OF
LAKE MICHIGAN STATE COMPANIES

Though far from complete, these company histories reflect their respective origins and contributions to the sweet baked products of Michigan, Illinois, Indiana and Wisconsin.

A.M. Todd
www.amtodd.com

Quality. Purity. Integrity. An unwavering belief in these principles inspired Albert May Todd, then a teenager, to found A.M. Todd Company in 1869. It was an era when mint essential oil from Michigan had a poor reputation thanks to widespread adulteration by unscrupulous vendors. Albert May's initiatives brought credibility to Michigan essential oils and early success to the A.M. Todd Company, now the world's oldest and largest supplier of American peppermint and spearmint oil.

During the last half century, A.M. Todd has grown far beyond its original mission. Today it is a global company and a natural resource for products and services used in the food industry, in botanically based therapeutics, in alternative and complementary medicines and in personal-care products. A.M. Todd expanded its global presence by developing farmlands and experimental plant stations in India and established A.M. Todd–United Kingdom to better serve European customers.

Argo Corn Starch
www.argostarch.com

Argo Cornstarch is a brand of Associated British Foods, a global food, ingredients and retail company headquartered in London. Its ingredients division is the world's second-largest producer of both sugar and baker's yeast and is a major producer of other ingredients, including emulsifiers, enzymes and lactose. ACH Food Companies is the American subsidiary.

Argo Cornstarch was started in 1892 in Illinois—more than one hundred years of quality in the amazing yellow box. While Kingsford's cornstarch (its rival) is still available in some parts of the country, Argo has become the largest-selling brand of 100 percent pure cornstarch in the United States.

Calumet Baking Powder
www.kraftfoods.com

Calumet Baking Powder Company was an American food company established in 1889 in Chicago, Illinois, by baking powder salesman William Monroe Wright. His newly formulated double-acting baking powder took its name from the Native American word for a peace pipe given to the lands now known as Calumet City, Illinois. Wright's company adopted an Indian head as its trademark.

In 1929, William Wright sold out to General Foods, and Calumet Baking Powder became one of General Foods' many name brands. General Foods merged with Kraft Foods in 1990.

Clabber Girl
www.clabbergirl.com

The Clabber Girl Corporation grew from the original business that was incorporated more than 150 years ago. Hulman & Company was established in Terre Haute, Indiana, in early 1850. Originally a wholesale grocery store, the business expanded into manufacturing with the addition of a storeroom and spice mill behind the store in 1869. The company continued to expand and, by 1879, was manufacturing a variety of products, including spices, coffees and baking powder, under many different brand names. By 1899, Clabber brand baking powder was introduced, and today the Clabber Girl brand, as renamed in 1923, is distributed nationwide and to many different countries around the world.

General Mills, Inc.
www.generalmills.com

General Mills is the United States' number one breakfast cereal maker (wrangling for the top spot every year with über-rival Kellogg's). But number one or not, the company has supermarket aisles full of kid-friendly morning-meal products. The company makes ice cream (Häagen-Dazs), canned soup (Progresso) and frozen dough products (Pillsbury), as well as its oldest ingredient, flour, for baking. General Mills, which produces yogurt under the Yoplait brand, bought a controlling stake in the world's second-largest yogurt maker for $1.2 billion in mid-2011.

Illinois congressman Robert Smith leased power rights to flour mills operating along Anthony Falls on the Mississippi River and helped found the Minneapolis Milling Company in 1856. Cadwallader C. Washburn, an attorney and lumber company owner in Wisconsin, purchased the company from Smith. This eventually became the Washburn-Crosby Company. After winning a gold medal for flour at an 1880 exposition, the company changed the name of its best flour to Gold Medal Flour.

Hodgson Mill, Inc.
www.hodgsonmill.com

When it comes to making whole grain products, Hodgson Mill is rock solid. The company touts its use of grinding stones (rather than the steel blades that the big companies use) to mill a variety of grains, including wheat, oats, rye and corn. The Missouri mill was built in 1837; company founder Alva Hodgson purchased the mill after its second rebuilding in 1882 in Illinois. Hodgson Mill products include flours, flax seed, couscous, cereals, bread and baking mixes, batters and non-gluten and soy products. It has added whole wheat and veggie dried pastas to its offerings, which are available at retail food outlets nationwide.

Hostess Brands
www.hostessbrands.com

After spending time driving a pound cake wagon pulled by a horse, Mr. James Dewar worked his way up to managing at the Continental Baking Company in River Forest, Illinois (later named Hostess Cake). He suggested a bakery item for Continental that would use the idle shortcake pans that had only been used during strawberry season. The 1930s Depression proved a challenge, as people were frugal in a slow economy. Mr. Dewar suggested injecting banana filling in the oblong golden cakes and naming them "Twinkie," after an advertisement he saw of "Twinkle Toe Shoes." Later the filling was changed to the present-day vanilla cream filling.

Hostess Brands (formerly Interstate Bakeries) is one of the largest wholesale bakers and distributors of fresh delivered bread and snack cakes in the United States. Hostess is the maker of the breads and cakes that have treated America for over a century—Twinkies, Ding Dongs, Ho Hos, Sno Balls, Donettes, Wonder Bread, Hostess Fruit Pies and many more. Recently the company launched Nature's Pride, a 100 percent all-natural, no-preservatives line of premium and traditional breads.

The company operates thirty-nine bakeries throughout the United States and employs about twenty-one thousand people. Hostess Brands is based in Dallas, Texas, with an operations center in Kansas City, Missouri. Hostess Brands also has about seven hundred bakery outlet stores.

Karo Syrup
www.karosyrup.com

In 1902, a chemist and expert syrup formulator named his syrup "Karo" after his wife, Caroline. The Corn Products Refining Company of New York and Chicago was formed, introducing Karo Light and Dark Corn Syrup. One hundred years later, Karo continues to lead in corn syrup production, introducing light corn syrup (fewer calories), as well as flavored corn syrups (brown sugar). Gluten-free and allergen-friendly are also new marketing features. Karo is a brand of ACH Food Companies, Inc (www.achfood.com).

ACH Food Companies products include edible oils, shortenings and other oil-based products, as well as food ingredients such as cornstarch, syrup, spices and cake decorations. The company has two divisions (consumer products and commercial products) that serve the retail, industrial food and food service markets. Its brands include the well-known Mazola Corn Oil, Argo Corn Starch, Fleischmann's Yeast and Karo Corn Syrup. ACH sells its products to customers in Canada, Mexico and the United States. It is a subsidiary of UK food, ingredient and retail giant Associated British Foods, which purchased ACH in 1995.

Kellogg Company
www.kelloggcompany.com

The Michigan-based Kellogg Company is in a constant battle for the number one spot in the U.S. cereal market with its main rival, General Mills. (General Mills' fiscal 2010 sales totaled about $14.8 billion, compared to Kellogg's $12.4 billion.) But Kellogg boasts many familiar brand names, including Kellogg's Corn Flakes, Frosted Flakes, Corn Pops and Rice Krispies. It has snacks and cookies (Keebler, Cheez-It and Famous Amos) along with convenience foods such as Eggo Waffles, and Nutri-Grain and Bear Naked cereal bars are also part of their food group. Its products are sold in more than 180 countries worldwide.

The company is also looking for continued growth from its vegetarian business, particularly its Morningstar Farms and Worthington Foods brands of meat alternatives. The veggie business has performed well as consumers look for healthier foods.

As head of the Battle Creek Toasted Corn Flake Company, Will Kellogg competed against forty-two cereal companies in Battle Creek and roared to the head of the pack with his innovative marketing ideas. A 1906 *Ladies' Home Journal* ad helped increase demand from 33 cases a day earlier that year to 2,900 a day by year's end. W.K. soon introduced Bran Flakes (1915), All-Bran (1916) and Rice Krispies (1928). International expansion began in Canada (1914) and followed in Australia (1924) and England (1938).

Kraft Foods, Inc.

www.kraft.com

Kraft Foods is the number one U.S. food company and number two worldwide (after Nestlé). Its North American unit boasts the world's largest-selling cheese brand (Kraft), cookie and cracker baker (Nabisco) and the milk-dunking favorite, Oreos. Its international business unit offers many of the same brands, plus national favorites. The Oscar Mayer, Kraft, Philadelphia, Maxwell House, Nabisco, Oreo, Jacobs, Milka, and LU brands all have revenues of at least $1 billion; more than fifty of its brands regularly hit the $100 million mark. Kraft's $19 billion offer for the acquisition of Cadbury became final in 2010.

The Kraft tale began in 1903 when James L. Kraft began delivering cheese to Chicago grocers. His four brothers joined in, forming the J.L. Kraft & Bros. Company in 1909. By 1914, the company had opened a cheese factory and was selling cheese across the United States. Kraft developed its first blended, pasteurized cheese the following year.

Kraft went public in 1924; four years later, it merged with Philadelphia cream cheese maker Phoenix and also created Velveeta cheese spread. In 1930, Kraft was bought by National Dairy, but its operations were kept separate. New and notable products included Miracle Whip salad dressing (1933), macaroni and cheese dinners (1937) and Parkay margarine (1940). In the decades that followed, Kraft expanded into foreign markets.

National Dairy became Kraftco in 1969 and then Kraft in 1976, hoping to benefit from its internationally known trademark. To diversify, Kraft merged with Dart Industries in 1980; Dart's subsidiaries (including Duracell batteries) and Kraft kept separate operations. With nonfood sales sagging, Dart and Kraft split up in 1986. Kraft kept its original lines and added Duracell (sold in 1988); the rest became Premark International. Tobacco giant Philip Morris bought Kraft in 1988 for $12.9 billion. The next year, Philip Morris joined Kraft with another unit, General Foods.

General Foods began when Charles Post, who marketed a wheat/bran health beverage, established the Postum Cereal Company in 1896; he expanded the firm with such cereals as Grape-Nuts and Post Toasties. The company went public in 1922. Postum bought the makers of Jell-O (1925), Baker's chocolate (1927), Log Cabin syrup (1927) and Maxwell House coffee (1928), and in 1929, it acquired control of General

Foods (owned by frozen vegetable pioneer Clarence Birdseye) and changed its own name to General Foods.

Philip Morris bought General Foods for $5.6 billion in 1985. The 1989 combination of Kraft and General Foods (the units still ran independently) created the largest U.S. food maker, Kraft General Foods.

Lesaffre Yeast Corporation
www.lesaffreyeastcorp.com/home

Red Star Yeast was founded in 1882 as Meadow Springs Distilling Company, in Milwaukee, Wisconsin. The merger of distilling and yeast making was a natural match. Not only was yeast needed for distillation, but grains could be also sold for animal feed. By 1885, 200,000 pounds of yeast was being sold to St. Louis, Chicago and, of course, Milwaukee. Blue Star, White Star and Battle Axe were a few early names of this yeast company. Prohibition shuttered distilling but fueled the demand for marketing yeast to bakers. The world wars and industrialization yielded new inventions and new ownership. Lesaffre Group acquired Red Star in 2001, continuing the tradition of the science of yeast.

Lloyd J. Harris Pie Company

West Michigan's unique microclimate created a fruit growing industry worth millions of dollars. In turn, the seemingly endless bushels of fruit ultimately led to the basket factory, a fruit grower's bank, the fruit exchange and the shipping industry. Rich products became involved with Lloyd Pies in Saugatuck, Michigan, in the late 1970s, selling the factory in the 1990s.

McNess
www.mcness.com

In 1908, Frank Furst and Fredrick McNess founded the Furst-McNess Company in Freeport, Illinois. Originally sold from horse-driven carriage, McNess exhibits the entrepreneurial spirit of quality food products. Home bakers purchase ingredients such as flavorings, extracts and oils.

Michigan Sugar Company
www.michigansugar.com

The Michigan Sugar Company was formed in 1906 when six independent, single-factory sugar beet companies merged. In 2002, it became a cooperative, owned by more than one thousand sugar beet growers. On October 1, 2004, the Monitor Sugar Beet Growers and Monitor Sugar's Bay City factory joined the cooperative. Beginning with the 2004 crop, the grower-owned cooperative processed all sugar produced in the state of Michigan.

Today, the company has four operating factories (Bay City, Caro, Croswell and Sebewaing) and three warehouse terminals located in Michigan and Ohio. It employs 940 year-round employees and 1,450 seasonal. Nearly $400 million is generated in direct economic activity annually in the local communities in which the company operates. Michigan Sugar Company is the third-largest beet sugar processor in the United States, annually producing nearly 1 billion pounds of sugar under the Pioneer and Big Chief brand names. "Locally Grown. Locally Owned."

Morton Salt
www.mortonsalt.com

Morton Salt is an American tradition, with roots that date back to 1848. Since then, based on consistent excellence and a constantly evolving product line that has passed the test of time and then some, the company has established itself as the trusted authority on salt. Morton introduced the country to the slogan "When it rains, it pours.™" It also introduced one of the most recognizable icons in the world: the Morton umbrella girl.

Since 1848, Morton has been America's leading producer of salt for water softening, ice control and agricultural and industrial uses, as well as for groceries. It is headquartered in Chicago, Illinois. In 1999, Morton was acquired by Philadelphia-based Rohm and Haas Company, Inc., and continued to serve as the Morton Division until October 1, 2009, when K+S successfully completed the acquisition of Morton Salt, Inc.

Nabisco
www.nabiscoworld.com/brands
www.kraftfoodscompany.com/brands/largest-brands/brands-n/nabisco.aspx

Nabisco dates its founding to 1898, a decade during which the bakery business underwent a major consolidation. Early in the decade, bakeries throughout the country were consolidated regionally into companies such as Chicago's American Biscuit and Manufacturing Company (which was formed from 40 midwestern bakeries in 1830), the New York Biscuit Company (consisting of 7 eastern bakeries) and the United States Baking Company. In 1898, the National Biscuit Company was formed from the combination of those three; the merger resulted in a company with 114 bakeries across the United States, headquartered in New York City. The "biscuit" in the name of the company is a British English and early American English term for cracker products.

Origins and Histories of Lake Michigan State Companies

The name Nabisco first appeared on a new sugar wafer product in 1901, but the corporate name did not change from National Biscuit Company to Nabisco, Inc., until 1971. Kraft acquired Nabisco in December 2000. Today, Nabisco's brands include some of the best-known cookies and crackers in the world, including Chips Ahoy!, Oreo and Ritz. The year 2001 found the headquarters in East Hanover, New Jersey. The company is a subsidiary of Illinois-based Kraft Foods. Nabisco's plant in Chicago is the largest bakery in the world, employing more than 1,500 workers and turning out some 320 million pounds of snack foods annually, including a variety of cookies.

New Rinkel Flour
www.newrinkelflour.com

Indiana's oldest water-powered mill has been family owned and operated for more than one hundred years since 1904.

Nielsen-Massey Vanillas
www.nielsenmassey.com

Nielsen-Massey Vanillas, located in Waukegan, Illinois, has been producing premium pure vanilla products since 1907. From its ever-popular Madagascar Bourbon Vanilla to custom blends and flavors created for specific customer needs, Nielsen-Massey has earned the reputation as a producer of fine vanillas worldwide. The Waukegan facility supplies vanilla products to North America, South America, Central America and the Pacific Rim. These products are shipped and sold locally as well as globally.

Penzeys
www.penzeys.com

In 1957, Ruth and Bill Penzey Sr. started a coffee and spice business in Milwaukee, Wisconsin. Later on, the Penzeys narrowed their business to focus solely on herbs and spices, calling it the Spice House. Throughout the 1990s, the mail-order business grew steadily, mostly by word of mouth. In 1994, the company branched out, opening the first Penzeys Spices store in Milwaukee, Wisconsin. By 2005, Penzeys had revenues of $22 million and operated twenty-seven retail stores in eighteen states.

PET Milk
www.petmilk.com

Evaporated milk was a popular product before refrigerators were common in homes, but it is now a niche product mainly used in baking and other recipes. PET realized this and transformed itself into a food products conglomerate through a series of acquisitions. Old El Paso and Progresso are two of its acquired brands.

1885—It starts with an idea of canning as a preservative in the small town of Highland, Illinois. After a $15,000 investment, the Helvetia Milk Condensing Company is born (later to be renamed PET).

1898—"Our PET" helps supply Teddy Roosevelt's Rough Riders and other American fighting troops with a safe and convenient source of milk in the Spanish-American War. At war's end, the troops scattered to their homes across the United States, with many remembering the high-quality milk and bringing it home to their families.

1914—Once again, the U.S. government places large orders of milk from PET to supply U.S. troops fighting overseas in World War I.

1929—In the midst of the Great Depression, PET becomes an important staple to American families and is able to expand its service to consumers with the creation of original recipes using PET products.

1941—PET is called on to supply GIs fighting in World War II, as well as the citizens at home. More recipes, specifically designed with ration limitations in mind, are created to help families get a wholesome diet.

1950—The combination of postwar prosperity and a baby boom results in more cans of PET Milk being sold than at any other time in the company's sixty-five-year history. PET also establishes its own test kitchens to develop and test new products and recipes.

1966—PET begins making "better for you" products, including a skim milk and a 99 percent fat-free evaporated skim milk.

Post
www.kraftfoods.com

Charles William Post spent time when he was ill at the Battle Creek Sanitarium, an Adventist Health Reform Institute managed by Dr. John Harvey Kellogg, who also hired his brother, Will Kellogg, to do various jobs at the facility. He was impressed with the new "healthy" foods that they were serving. His first ideas encompassed coffee substitutes and breakfast cereals.

The coffee substitute in 1897 had annual sales of $840,000. He then began to formulate a cereal, Granula, known today as Grape-Nuts. Post's advertising, marketing through coupons, recipe books and contests offered his product to the "everyday man and woman." This method of product delivery was new and different for the early 1900s.

Quaker Oats
www.quakeroats.com/home

"A figure of a man in Quaker garb"—this is how Quaker Oats registered the first trademark for breakfast cereal. Henry Seymour and William Heston began this cereal company, but when it became bankrupt, they sold it to Henry Crowell in 1881. The Quaker Mill, in Ravenna, Ohio, began advertising in magazines and was the first to portray a recipe on the exterior of a box (oatmeal bread). Oatmeal battles occurred, with the eventual rise of Crowell and his new partner, Stuart, producing wheat cereals, farina, hominy, cornmeal, baby food and animal feed. By 1911, they owned one-quarter of the oat mills east of the Rocky Mountains. Quaker acquired further brand-name companies like Aunt Jemima in the 1950s but diversified in the 1980s into beverages and pet foods. The twenty-first century finds the company involved with energy drinks and energy bars. By the way, some energy bars do include oatmeal! Today, Chicago, Illinois, is the headquarters for Quaker Oats.

Between 1901 and 1911, many of the industry's leading producers, then operating under the umbrella of groups such as the American Cereal Company and the Great Western Cereal Company, were absorbed by the Quaker Oats Company. This Chicago-based giant grew steadily, making big business out of oatmeal. By the close of the twentieth century, it was selling more than $5 billion annually from a diverse range of products, including cereals, pastas and Gatorade sports drinks.

Sara Lee
www.saralee.com

Sara Lee was eight years old when Charlie Lubin, a bakery entrepreneur, decided to name his new line of cheesecakes after his daughter. The name of the business was changed to Kitchens of Sara Lee and had "fresh" routes throughout Chicago. His company was purchased in 1956 by Consolidated Foods, whereupon Mr. Lubin continued to serve as a senior executive for many years. In 1985, Consolidated Foods changed its name to Sara Lee Corporation. Although Sara Lee has never had a management role at the corporation, she appeared in some television advertisements for the bakery products. In her words, her father told her that the product "had to be perfect because he was naming it after me." Today, Sara Lee is a philanthropist who spends most of her time supporting the education and advancement of women in science.

Swans Down Cake Flour

www.swansdown.com

Swans Down is the oldest and most respected name in scratch baking. The Igleheart brothers opened their first mill in Evansville, Indiana, in 1856. It was purchased by Postum in 1926. Today, it is owned by William B. Reily & Company, founded in 1902 by its namesake. Originally, the company distributed and roasted coffee, and in 1985, it purchased Swans Down Cake Flour from General Foods, part of the Post Company. The 1980s brought acquisitions of spices and teas, including the famous Luzianne name.

Uneeda Biscuit

www.kraftfoodscompany.com

The tale of the Uneeda biscuit boy (found on the early company products) is the story of early American advertising boiled down to a single parable that just happens to be real history. In the early 1890s, there were hundreds of hometown bakers putting out generic crackers in barrels with plain cookies in square shipping boxes. Mother would say, "George, here's a paper bag. Go down to the store and fill this with crackers." Uneeda was one of the first mass-marketed products outside of its region, due to the "sanitary packaging" it promoted as being a step above the cracker barrel in terms of health and convenience. Chicago's American Biscuit and Manufacturing Company, which was formed from forty bakeries, started a trend of bakery consolidation, eventually merging with the National Biscuit Company, which launched the first prepackaged biscuit, Uneeda, with the slogan "Lest you forget, we say it yet, Uneeda Biscuit." In 2009 (after 110 years), Nabisco discontinued the Uneeda biscuit out of concern that the product was not as profitable as others.

Sweet Fairs and Festivals

Many communities still converge today to celebrate their heritages with contests, food, street fairs, exhibits, music, parades and more. Inventions, creativity and the entrepreneurial spirit still propel these contemporary events. Sweet baked items have always been popular segments in these celebrations. Although this list is far from complete, it exemplifies the strength of sweet traditions through many gatherings.

Festivals

Blueberry Festival
Plymouth, Indiana
An event filled with varying activities: parade, softball, blueberry eating and baking, too.

Cherry Festival
Traverse City, Michigan
About 75 percent of the country's tart cherries hail from Michigan, where cherry growers in the Traverse Bay area have held a "blessing of the blossoms" ceremony each spring since the early twentieth century. This humble ceremony has morphed into a massive weeklong festival packed with more than 150 events, including a cherry pit spit contest.

Cranberry Festival
Warrens, Wisconsin
Wisconsin hosts no less than five cranberry festivals. The cranberry is Wisconsin's official state fruit, and the best place to celebrate these ruby fruits is here in the Cranberry Capital of Wisconsin.

Maple Syrup Festival
Vermontville, Michigan
They have something for everyone: mid-America rides, talent shows, arts and crafts, flea markets, two parades, petting zoos, princess pageants and arm wrestling. Syrup producers are located throughout the village selling syrup, candies, crème and the ever-popular maple syrup cotton candy.

Pasty Festival
Calumet, Michigan
Nicknamed Copper Town, this Upper Peninsula town celebrates pies baked with meat, vegetables and sometimes fruits with a parade, a bake-off and games.

Persimmon Festival
Mitchell, Indiana
This exotic-sounding fruit often is associated with Japan, but persimmon trees are plentiful in southern Indiana. Now in its sixty-fifty year (as of 2011), the festival includes a carnival, a parade, tournaments and the always popular persimmon pudding contest.

Pumpkin Festival
Morton, Illinois
The pumpkin harvest is celebrated with carnival rides, punkin'-chuckin' contests, arts and crafts and pumpkins of all sizes cooked in various ways. No wonder this is called the "Pumpkin Capital of the World."

Strawberry Festival
Cedarburg, Wisconsin
Pie eating, strawberry brats, strawberry wine and berry bob contests should be enough to lure you to this historic avenue in a town half an hour outside of Milwaukee.

Sugar Festival
Sebewaing, Michigan
Sweet beginnings for this festival date to 1964. A Sugar Queen and court are part of the celebrations, along with arts and crafts and sweet tastings, too.

STATE FAIRS

Indiana State Fair
Indianapolis, Indiana
The year 2011 marks 155 years of the Indiana State Fair. In 1852, at the urging of the governor, the state fair was formed to promote Indiana's agricultural products.

Illinois State Fair
Springfield, Illinois
In 1853, the first Illinois State Fair charged twenty-five cents for admission. Early fairs exhibited farmers sharing "notes" and advice on agriculture. Fairs also moved to various locations throughout Illinois, eventually settling on its permanent capital, Springfield.

Michigan State Fair
Detroit, Michigan
Claimed to be the oldest U.S. state fair, first held in 1849, the last fair was in 2009 due to budget cuts. Beginning as a fair to promote agriculture, it later also exhibited the partnerships of industry and agriculture working together.

Upper Peninsula State Fair
Escanaba, Michigan
Organized by farmers, this second Michigan State Fair opened in 1928. Today, in 2011, it continues to be the only Michigan State Fair without any financing from the State of Michigan.

Wisconsin State Fair
West Allis, Wisconsin
In 1851, the first fair for Wisconsin was held in Janesville. Agricultural exhibits reigned strong, but with the partnering of the dairy farmers and the Wisconsin Baker's Association in the 1920s, cream-filled puffs became a sought-after commodity, and they still are!

BIBLIOGRAPHY

Algren, Nelson, and David E. Schoonover. *America Eats*. Iowa City: University of Iowa, 1992.

All Business. "Flour and Other Grain Mill Products." http://www.allbusiness.com/food-kindred-products/grain-mill-products-flour/3779250-3.html.

America's Best History. americasbesthistory.com/abhtimeline1900.html.

American Egg Board. "Egg Industry." www.aeb.org/egg-industry.

American Heritage Magazine. www.americanheritage.com.

American Immigration Law Foundation. "The Story of Italian Immigration." www.ailf.org/awards/benefit2004/ahp04essay.asp.

A.M. Todd. www.amtodd.com.

Anderson, Jean. *American Century Cookbook*. New York: Clarkson Potter, 1997.

Answers.com. "Cereal Grains." www.answers.com/topic/cereal-grains-1.

———. "Pumpkin." www.answers.com/topic/pumpkin.

———. "Sugar Industry." www.answers.com/topic/sugar-industry-1.

Apricots' History. http://www.apricot-oil.com/en/apricots/apricot_history.html.

Argo & Kingsford's Corn Starch. www.argostarch.com/index.html.

Armstrong, William John. Michigan Peach History. http://michiganpeach.org/michpeachhistory.html.

Baker Library. "PET Incorporated—Lehman Brothers Collection." Bloomberg Center. www.library.hbs.edu/hc/lehman/chrono.html?company=pet_incorporated.

Baking Buyer magazine, April 2011. Kansas City, Missouri.

Baking History. http://bakinghistory.wordpress.com.

Beetz, Kirk. "Cereal Grains." Answers.com. http://www.answers.com/topic/cereal-grains-1.

Bellis, Mary. "The History of Cheesecake and Cream Cheese." Inventors. http://inventors.about.com/od/cstartinventions/a/Cheesecake.htm.

———. "The History of Jello." Inventors. http://inventors.about.com/library/inventors/bljello.htm.

———. "Who Invented Peanut Butter?" Inventors. http://inventors.about.com/library/inventors/blpeanutbutter.htm.

Bilingsley, Sarah, and Amy Treadwell. "Classic Chocolate Whoopie & Classic Marshmallow." *Whoopie Pies*. San Francisco, CA: Chronicle LLC, 2010.

Boston University, Physics Department. "Index of /~redner/projects/population/cities." http://physics.bu.edu/~redner/projects/population/cities.

Bread Baking. "War Bread—World War I White Bread—Recipe for War Bread." http://breadbaking.about.com/od/yeastbreads/r/warbread.htm.

Brittannica. www.brittannica.com.

California Rare Fruit Growers, Inc. "Pawpaw or Michigan Banana." Holoweb, Inc., 1996. www.holoweb.com/cannon/pawpawor.htm.

Callahan, Carol. *Prairie Avenue Cookbook: Recipes and Recollections from Prominent 19th-century Chicago Families*. Carbondale: Southern Illinois University Press, 1993.

Carriage House. "History." www.carriagehouseharbor.com/history.html.

Cheesemaking. www.cheesemaking.com.

College of Agricultural, Consumer and Environmental Sciences, University of Illinois. "Nut Growing Table of Contents." www.aces.uiuc.edu/vista/html_pubs/NUTGROW/nuthome.html.

College of Agriculture and Natural Resources, Michigan State University. www.canr.msu.edu.

Commodity Futures Seasonal Analysis for Traders. www.commodityseasonals.com.

Communal Cuisines: Community Cookbooks, 1877–1960. Urbana-Champagne, IL: University of Illinois, 2011.

Corn Refiners Association. "History." www.corn.org/about-2/history.

Crisco. "About Crisco." www.crisco.com/About_Crisco.

Culinary Institute of America. "The Story of the World's Premier Culinary College." www.ciachef.edu/about/history.asp.

Current Captivating Copper Country Cooking. Compiled by a First Presbyterian Church Circle in Houghton, Michigan. Calumet, MI: Keewenah Printing Company, 1930s.

David Thompson Things. "Delicious Old Time Voyageur Recipes." www.davidthompsonthings.com/VoyRecipes.htm.

Davis, William C. *A Taste for War*. Mechanicsburg, PA: Stackpole, 2003.

Detroit Salt Company. The Kissner Group. www.detroitsalt.com/about-detroit-salt-company.html.

Duis, Perry. *Challenging Chicago, Coping with Everyday Life, 1837–1920*. Champaign: University of Illinois Press, 1998.

Eight Hundred Proved Pecan Recipes. N.p.: Keystone Pecan Research Laboratory, 1925.

Encyclopedia of Chicago. "Food Processing: Local Market." www.encyclopedia.chicagohistory.org/pages/468.html.

Epicurious. "Sweet Ricotta Pastries." http://epicurious.com.

Facts About. "Facts about the History of Indiana." www.facts-about.org.uk/history-us-state-indiana.htm.

———. "Facts about the History of Michigan." www.facts-about.org.uk/history-us-state-michigan.htm.

Farmer, Fannie. *The Original Fannie Farmer 1896 Cookbook*. Baltimore, MD: Ottenheimer, 1896.

Fertig, Judith M. *Prairie Home Cooking: 400 Recipes that Celebrate the Bountiful Harvests, Creative Cooks, and Comforting Foods of the American Heartland*. Boston, MA: Harvard Common, 1999.

Food. www.food.com.

Food Export Association of the Midwest USA and Food Export USA-Northeast. www. foodexport.org.

Food Timeline. http://foodtimeline.org.

4-H History Preservation Progam. http://www.4-hhistorypreservation.com.

Funding Universe. "Keebler Foods Company." www.fundinguniverse.com/company-histories/ Keebler-Foods-Company-Company-History.html.

Gisslen, Wayne. *Professional Baking, Fourth Edition: Instructor's Guide*. Hoboken, NJ: John Wiley, 2005.

Goliath. "US: Kellogg Acquires Cookie Manufacturers." goliath.ecnext.com/coms2/gi_0199-8352583/US-Kellogg-acquires-cookie-manufacturers.html.

Good Housekeeping's Cake Book. Chicago, IL: Consolidated Book, 1958.

Gordon, Donald. *Growing Fruit in the Upper Midwest*. Minneapolis: University of Minnesota, 1991.

The Greenwood Encyclopedia of American Regional Cultures: The Midwest. http://www.credoreference. com/entry.do?pp=1&id=9630191.

Greweling, Peter P. *Chocolates and Confections: Formula, Theory, and Technique for the Artisan Confectioner*. Hoboken, NJ: John Wiley and Sons, 2007.

Harveson, Robert. "History of Sugarbeet Production and Use." Crop Watch. http:// cropwatch.unl.edu/web/sugarbeets/sugarbeet_history.

Harzig, Christiane. "Germans." Encyclopedia of Chicago. http://encyclopedia.chicagohistory. org/pages/512.html.

Hess, Elam G. *800 Proved Pecan Recipes: Their Place in the Menu*. N.p.: Innes & Sons, 1925.

Heyman, Patricia A., and Alan H. Roer. *American Regional Cooking: A Culinary Journey*. Upper Saddle River, NJ: Pearson Prentice Hall, 2009.

Historical Boys' Clothing. "World War I—United States Food Administration." http://histclo. com/essay/war/ww1/cou/us/food/w1cus-usfa.html.

History Cook. http://www.historycook.com/game/shortcake.htm

Home Cooking. "Canned Milk History—Evaporated and Sweetened Condensed Milk." http://homecooking.about.com/od/milkproducts/a/canmilkhistory.htm.

Home Cooking Recipes. "Pecan History." http://homecooking.about.com/od/foodhistory/a/ pecanhistory.htm?p=1.

Hoovers. www.hoovers.com.

Internet Archive. "Full Text of 'Johnny Appleseed's Rhymes.'" www.archive.org/stream/ johnnyappleseeds00snidiala/johnnyappleseeds00snidiala_djvu.txt.

Inventors. "The Kitchen—History of Kitchen Appliances." http://inventors.about.com/od/ kstartinventions/a/kitchen.htm.

Jewish Virtual Library. "Jews in Early Indiana." www.jewishvirtuallibrary.org/jsource/vjw/ Indiana.html.

Jones, Evan. *American Food: The Gastronomic Story*. N.p.: Dutton, 1975.

Journal of Antiques and Collectibles. "Pie Crusts, from Meat to Fruit." Hearth to Hearth Article. (November 2000; July 2011). http://journalofantiques.com/hearthnov.htm.

Kaercher, Dan. *Taste of the Midwest: 12 States, 101 Recipes, 150 Meals, 8,207 Miles and Millions of Memories*. Guildford, CT: Insider's Guide, 2006.

Karo Syrup. "Recipes Search Results." http://karosyrup.com/recipe_details_text.asp?id=485.

Kellogg Company. www.kelloggcompany.com.

Kentucky State University Cooperative Extension Program. "Cooking with Pawpaws." www.hort.purdue.edu/newcrop/ksu-pawpaw/cooking.html.

Kosher Celiac Cooking. www.kosherceliaccookery.com.

Kraft Foods Company. "Kraft History." www.kraftfoodscompany.com/about/history/index.aspx.

The Lewis and Clark Trail. www.lewisandclarktrail.com.

Lukins, Sheila. "Almond Sour Cream Cheesecake Recipe." *The New Basics Cookbook*. Ed. Julee Rosso. New York: Workman, 1989.

McKee, Gwen, and Barbara Moseley. *Best of the Best from Michigan: Selected Recipes from Michigan's Favorite Cookbooks*. Brandon, MS: Quail Ridge Press, 1996.

Michigan State Historical Preservation Objects. "The Michigan Stove." www.mcgi.state.mi.us/hso/sites/15650.htm.

Michigan State University Department of Geography. "The French Explorers." www.geo.msu.edu/geogmich/french_explorers.html.

Michigan State University Libraries. "Feeding America." Digital and Multimedia Center. http://digital.lib.msu.edu/projects/cookbooks/coldfusion/display.cfm?TitleNo=30.

Michigan Sugar Company. "Company History." www.michigansugar.com/about/history.php.

Midwest Living Magazine. "Apple-Pear Praline Pie." www.midwestliving.com/recipe/pies/apple-pear-praline-pie.

Milwaukee Public Museum. "Gardens and Farming—Indian Country Wisconsin." www.mpm.edu/wirp/ICW-31.html.

Mondale, Clarence. "The History of the Upper Midwest: An Overview." Pioneering the Upper Midwest. http://memory.loc.gov/ammem/umhtml/umessay4.html.

Montana Wheat & Barley Committee. "Kernel Diagram." wbc.agr.mt.gov/consumers/diagram_kernel.html.

Morrison, Abraham. *The Baking Powder Controversy*. Volume 2. books.google.com/books?id=fIb ZAAAAMAAJ&pg=PA1628&lpg=PA1628&dq=.

Morton® Salt. "Heritage." www.mortonsalt.com/heritage/index.html.

Nakate, Shashank. "History of Strawberries." Buzzle Web Portal. www.buzzle.com/articles/history-of-strawberries.html.

National Historic Cheesemaking Center. "Cheese History." http://nationalhistoriccheesemakingcenter.org/Cheesemaking-History.aspx.

National Pecan Shellers Association. www.ilovepecans.org.

New World Encyclopedia. "Manifest Destiny." www.newworldencyclopedia.org/entry/Manifest_Destiny.

Non-Timber Forest Products. www.sfp.forprod.vt.edu.

Nutrition and You. "Persimmon Fruit Nutrition Facts and Health Benefits." www.nutrition-and-you.com/persimmon-fruit.html.

Ocean Spray. www.oceanspray.com.

Ohio Pawpaw Festival. www.ohiopawpawfest.com.

Old-Fashioned Persimmon Recipes. Nashville, IN: Bear Wallow, 1978.

Original Cream Puffs. "History." www.originalcreampuffs.com/history.htm.

Oso Ono: Fried Dessert Dough. "All About Johnnycakes." http://home.comcast.net/~osoono/ethnicdoughs/johnny-cake/johnny-cake.htm.

Owens, Frances E. *Mrs. Owens' Cook Book and Useful Household Hints*. Chicago, IL: Owens Publishing Company, 1884–85.

Oxford Dictionary of National Biography. "Henry Jones." www.oxforddnb.com/index/74/101074330.

Parker, Hilary. "A Sweet Problem: Princeton Researchers Find that High-Fructose Corn Syrup Prompts Considerably More Weight Gain." News at Princeton, Princeton University, March 22, 2010.

Peemoeller, Lynn. "Heritage Apples." Edible Chicago. http://www.ediblecommunities.com/chicago/fall-2009/heritage-apples.htm.

Perl, Lila. *Red-flannel Hash and Shoo-Fly Pie*. N.p.: World Pub., 1965.

Persimmonpudding.com. "Persimmon Pudding." www.persimmonpudding.com.

PET Milk. "History of PET Milk." www.petmilk.com/history.

Plains Humanities Alliance Digital Initiatives. "The Great Plains During World War II." http://plainshumanities.unl.edu/homefront/rationing?section=homefront.

Quaker Oats. www.quakeroats.com.

Recipe Curio. "Swans Down Wartime Cake Recipes." http://recipecurio.com/swans-down-wartime-cakes.

Recipes4Us. www.recipes4us.co.uk.

Rodriguez, Carlos Manuel, and Matthew Boyle. "Bimbo Buys Sara Lee Bakery Unit—SFGate." Featured Articles from SFGate. November 10, 2010; July 21, 2011. articles.sfgate.com/2010-11-10/business/24824084_1_sara-lee-s-north-american-christopher-growe-grupo-bimbo.

Rombauer, Irma. *The Joy of Cooking*. New York: Penguin Putnam Group, 1953.

Shuman, Carrie. *Favorite Dishes: A Columbian Autograph Souvenir*. Chicago, IL: R.R. Donnelly & Sons, 1893.

Slow Food International. "About Us." www.slowfood.com/international/1/about-us?-session=query_session:631F9CB81168f0A5B3GLD7739BA0.

Slow Food USA. www.slowfoodusa.org.

Smithsonian.com. "The Man Who Invented Elsie, the Borden Cow." www.smithsonianmag.com/science-nature/object_sep99.html.

Smucker's. http://smuckers.com.

Sokolov, Raymond A. *Fading Feast: A Compendium of Disappearing American Regional Foods*. New York: Farrar Straus Giroux, 1981.

State of Michigan. "Brief History of Michigan's State Fair." http:// www.michigan.gov/dnr/0,4570,7-153-54463_18670_18793-53223--,00.html.

State of Michigan. www.michigan.gov.

Stewart, Elizabeth. *Lessons in Cookery: Food Economy.* New York: Rand McNally and Company, 1918. http://books.google.com/books?id=CpgBAAAAYAAJ&pg=PA152&lpg=PA152&dq=lessons+in+cookery,+frances+stewart,+rennet&source=.

Time. "A Brief History of State Fairs—Photo Essays." www.time.com/time/photogallery/0,29307,1916488,00.html.

The Twinkies Cookbook: An Inventive and Unexpected Recipe Collection from Hostess. Berkeley, CA: Ten Speed, 2006.

BIBLIOGRAPHY

Undersander, D.J., L.H. Smith, A.R. Kaminski, K.A. Kelling and J.D.Doll. "Sorghum—Forage." Alternative Field Crops Manual. University of Wisconsin Cooperative Extension Program. www.hort.purdue.edu/newcrop/afcm/forage.html.

USDA Food Safety and Inspection Service. "Egg Products and Food Safety." www.fsis.usda.gov/Fact_Sheets/Egg_Products_and_Food_Safety/index.asp.

U.S. Environmental Protection Agency. "Food Irradiation | Radiation Protection." www.epa.gov/radiation/sources/food_irrad.html.

U.S. Highbush Blueberry Council. www.blueberry.org.

Visit Gettysburg. "Mary Todd Lincoln Cake." www.visit-gettysburg.com/mary-todd-lincoln-cake.html.

Visit Wisconsin Rapids. "Wisconsin Rapids Area Convention & Visitors Bureau: Cranberry Facts." http://www.visitwisrapids.com/printable.jsp?nid=18.

Walnut Council. "Botanical Description." www.walnutcouncil.org/botanical_description.htm.

Weaver, William. *Pennsylvania Dutch Cooking*. New York: Artabras, 1997.

Web Exhibits. "Explore the History and Making of Butter." www.webexhibits.org/butter/index.html.

What's Cooking America. "Danish Kringle, Kringle Recipe, History of Kringles, How to Make Kringles, Danish Kringle Recipe, Bread Machine Recipes." http://whatscookingamerica.net/Bread/Kringle.htm.

———. "History of Cookies." http://whatscookingamerica.net/History/CookieHistory.htm.

Wheat Foods Council. www.wheatfoods.org.

Wikipedia. "Henry Jones (baker)." http://en.wikipedia.org/wiki/Henry_Jones_(baker).

———. "Maple Syrup." en.wikipedia.org/wiki/maple_syrup.

———. "Milwaukee Area Technical College." http://en.wikipedia.org/wiki/Milwaukee_Area_Technical_College.

Wisconsin Cranberry Museum and Cranberry Products. www.discovercranberries.com.

World History International. "Hispanic Americans." http://history-world.org/hispanics.htm.

Yetter, Elizabeth. "Bread Baking." About.com. http://breadbaking.about.com/od/yeastbreads/r/warbread.htm.

Zeitlin, Richard H. "Germans in Wisconsin." For the State Historical Society of Madison, Wisconsin, 1977. www.dwave.net/~dhuehner/germanwis.html.

RECIPE INDEX

INDEX

ABOUT THE AUTHOR

My passion for food, specifically sweet baked goods, began at a young age. Baking at home transformed into working at bake shops, restaurants and, eventually, fine dining establishments. I earned a BA while I continued work in hotels and restaurants, with an added AAS in culinary arts—I finally had found my passion. More than twenty years in the food industry inspired me to move toward teaching and writing about sweet baked goods. As a Certified Culinary Educator (CCE, American Culinary Federation), I continually create new classes, hence why I have scoured books appropriate for my students and personal interests. It is also here where I have found a void in information. An in-depth training seminar for the Chicago's historical Prairie Avenue homes laid the foundation for an interest in middle states history. As a fifth-generation Chicagoan, I am honored to tell the stories of immigrants' baking traditions combined with rich company histories, as well as the lore of contemporary and historical recipes.

Also by Jenny Lewis:

Food columnist, *Daily Southtown Newspaper*, Chicago, Illinois, 2004–6 and August 2008. Monthly "Baking Bits" columnist for 100,000-circulation daily newspaper; column included a recipe with a baking industry perspective.
Writer/contributor, "Smooth as Ganache," *Chef Educator* magazine, summer 2010.
Writer/contributor, "Herbs, Spices, Minerals, and Flavoring Agents," in Garlough, Robert. *Modern Foodservice Purchasing*. New York: Delmar, 2011.

www.ingramcontent.com/pod-product-compliance
Lightning Source LLC
Chambersburg PA
CBHW082145150426
42812CB00076B/1912